This book may be recalled before the above date.

This book may be recall...

Real Language Series

General Editors:

Jennifer Coates, Roehampton Institate, London,
Jenny Cheshire, Universities of Fribourg and Neuchâtel,
and
Euan Reid, Institute of Education, University of London

Titles published in the series:

Text, Discourse and Context: Representations of Poverty in Britain

Editors: *Ulrike H. Meinhof and Kay Richardson*

LONGMAN
London and New York

Longman Group Limited,
Longman House, Burnt Mill,
Harlow, Essex CM20 2JE, England
and Associated Companies throughout the world.

Published in the United States of America
by Longman Publishing, New York

First published 1994

ISBN 0–582–10214–6 csd
ISBN 0–582–10213–8 ppr 1001203343

British Library Cataloguing-in-Publication Data
A catalogue record for this book is
available from the British Library

Library of Congress Cataloging-in-Publication Data
Text, discourse and context : representations of poverty in Britain /
    editors, Ulrike Meinhof and Kay Richardson.
        p. cm. — (Real language series)
        Includes bibliographical references and index.
    ISBN 0–582–10214–6 (csd). – ISBN 0–582–10213–8 (pbk)
    1. English language—Great Britain—Discourse analysis.
    2. English language—Social aspects—Great Britain. 3. Poverty—Great
    Britain—Public opinion. 4. Poverty—Great Britain—Terminology. 5.
    English language—Syntax. I. Meinhof, Ulrike Hanna. 1947–
    II. Richardson, Kay, 1955– . III. Series.
        PE1422.T49 1994
        401'.41'0941—dc20   93–50744
                                                                CIP

Set 8 in Sabon

Produced by Longman Singapore Publishers (Pte) Ltd
Printed in Singapore

Contents

Contributors

Dr Roger Hewitt is a Research Lecturer in the Social Science Research Unit, Institute of Education, University of London. His research has been concerned with orality; ethnicity; race and language; and more recently with racial harassment. His primary methodological orientation has been within ethnography and discourse analysis. He is best known for his book *White Talk Black Talk: Inter-racial Friendship and Communication Amongst Adolescents*, Cambridge University Press, 1986.

Gunther Kress is interested in the complex interrelations of social and cultural matters and their representations in the form of signs. He has published in the areas of critical Discourse Analysis and Social Semiotics: with Robert Hodge *Language as Ideology* (Routledge 1993) and *Social Semiotics* (Polity Press 1989); *Linguistic Processes in Sociocultural Practice* (Oxford University Press 1989); *Learning to Write* (Routledge 1993); and he is currently working on a book *The Design of Visual Communication* (to be published by Routledge) with Theo van Leeuwen, with whom he has published *Reading Images* (Deakin University Press 1990). He is Professor of Education/English at the Institute of Education, University of London.

Dr Ulrike H. Meinhof is a lecturer in German linguistics at the University of Manchester, and Visiting Professor in Language in Education at the University of Göteborg in Sweden. Her research is in applied linguistics, with a strong interest in social semiotics. She has published a range of articles and books on language teaching as well as on discourse analysis with particular emphasis on media texts. Recent work on the genre of television news, in particular, has led to textbooks such as *ITN World News* (with M. Bergman, OUP 1993), with others in preparation; articles in journals and books such as *Die Neueren Sprachen, British Papers in Applied Linguistics*, and *Media texts: Authors and Readers* (D. Graddol & O. Boyd-Barett (eds.) 1993, Multilingual Matters), and the development of an interactive video program for teaching foreign language television news *Interactive News*.

Kay Richardson is Lecturer in Communication Studies in the School of Politics and Communication Studies, University of Liverpool. Her main interests are in the study of political discourse, the politics of language and in television audience research. Publications include *Nuclear Reactions* (with John Corner and Natalie Fenton, John Libbey 1990) and *Researching Language* (with Deborah Cameron, Elizabeth Frazer, Penelope Harvey and M. B. H. Rampton, Routledge 1992), as well as articles in *Text, Multilingua, Media, Culture and Society*.

Dr Brian V. Street is Senior Lecturer in Social Anthropology at the University of Sussex and Visiting Professor of Education in the Graduate School of Education, University of Pennsylvania. He undertook anthropological fieldwork in Iran during the 1970s, and has since worked in the USA, Britain, and South Africa. He has written and lectured extensively on literacy practices from both a theoretical and an applied perspective. He is best known for *Literacy in Theory and Practice* (CUP 1985) and has recently published an edited volume *Cross-Cultural Approaches to Literacy* (CUP 1993). A collection of his articles *Social Literacies*, will be published shortly by Longman. He was recently guest editor for a special issue of the *Journal for Research in Reading* (vol. 16, no. 2, 1994: UK Reading Association) on 'The New Literacy Studies'.

His latest research, supported by an ESRC award and in collaboration with D. Sheridan, involved investigating everyday writing practices in the UK. This involved interviewing and reading material from self-selected adults around the country who write responses to questions on social and personal issues for the Mass-Observation Archive at the University of Sussex. A number of publications based on this work are planned.

Acknowledgements

We are grateful to the following for permission to reproduce copyright material:

Solo Syndication & Literary Agency for extracts & headlines from *Daily Mail* 26.4.91, 5.92. and *Evening Standard* 2.5.91; Express Newspapers Ltd for extracts & headlines from *Daily Express* 8.4.91, 27.4.91, 3.5.91 (including Figure 1.1), 2.5.92; Guardian News Services for extracts & headlines from *The Guardian* 26.5.91, 3.5.91, 7.5.91 & *Weekend Guardian* and Victoria Brittain for Figure 2.1, April 20–21, 1991; Mirror Group Newspapers for extracts & headlines from *Mirror* 8.4.91, 30.4.91, 2.5.91, 3.5.91; Newspaper Publishing plc for an extract & headlines from *Independent* 24.3.91, 26.4.91, 29.4.91, 27.4.93; Ewan MacNaughton Associates for headlines from *Daily Telegraph* 24.4.91, 27.4.91; Times Newspapers Ltd for headline from *The Times* 27.4.91. © Times Newspapers Ltd. 1991.

Introduction

Ulrike Meinhof and Kay Richardson

Reality is mediated through representations. In our increasingly complex post-industrial societies, the mass media are a crucial source of such representations – a provider of texts to be negotiated by their readers and viewers. Making sense of the world we live in can be seen, in part, as a 'textual practice', where representations of many kinds and at many levels interact in the consciousness of individual subjects. The purpose of this book is to explore in detail some aspects of this interpretative work. We draw upon a range of different approaches within the social sciences, by no means confining ourselves to a single academic tradition. The conceptual and methodological issues that interest us are ones which cut across orthodox disciplinary boundaries. To ensure a degree of coherence across the various contributions we have selected a single theme, and for reasons we give below, we have chosen 'poverty in Britain' as our substantive topic. The texts that we shall be discussing in the chapters which follow are selections from a single corpus.

How did this volume come about, and why do we think it belongs in this Real Language Series? The series occupies a space within the domain of 'applied linguistics', many of whose practitioners have little confidence in what is still widely seen as the intellectual project of linguistics: the study of one or more rule-governed 'layer', such as the phonology, morphology, syntax, semantics or pragmatics of a specific language, or of language as a universal phenomenon. Those who attend applied linguistics conferences rarely see themselves as applying a secure conceptual framework, or body of knowledge, to a problem area. To engage in applied linguistics is, very often, to be concerned with the re-conceptualization of language and its relation to psychological and social reality. That is certainly the case with the present volume. For us, its authors, the object of inquiry is not language in the narrowly linguistic sense at all; for one thing, images are just as important to us as words and clauses. For another, and most importantly, we are concerned with meaning – social meaning, and its construction and negotiation by readers and viewers. It was in this spirit that we initially drafted a book proposal with the provisional title 'Viewing the poor: a multidisciplinary approach to representations of poverty in Britain', thus foregrounding the multidisciplinary nature of the exercise. What we were proposing was a book in which the various chapters, though concerned with the same issue, poverty in Britain, and the same set of texts, offered distinctive but complementary ways of approaching those texts and ways of getting meaning 'from' those texts. In large measure this book does fulfil that aim. The emphasis is thus principally on meaning – the making of meaning in the making of text, and in the reading – i.e. remaking – of text. This gives the book a methodological feel, though not, we hope, in a narrow sense, for it does not describe and exemplify a set of formal 'methods' for the analysis of texts. Its concerns are broad ones, dealing as much with questions of the social practices of making meaning, with epistemology, as with technical analytical matters.

The five main chapters of this book were devised and written up independently by the authors to whom they are respectively attributed. Each of us agreed to contribute to the overall project by providing a particular kind of reading, or a kind of investigation which is distinctive of that person's approach, and which would thus add a substantively different perspective in comparison with the other chapters. However, any notion that we each belonged to clearcut disciplinary or subdisciplinary traditions with markedly different epistemological assumptions, conceptual agendas and/or analytic procedures quickly disappeared, as we discussed amongst ourselves the similarities and differences between the work that we were producing. On the one hand, the authors appear here together because they share a broadly compatible theoretical and political approach. On the other hand, all the authors are committed to cross-, inter-, multidisciplinary modes of working. In consequence, there is a considerable degree of convergence in the intellectual direction of the various contributions. That convergence is not complete – we are still some way from producing a single theoretical framework with a defined place for each of our different approaches. What is more, we are not certain at this stage that such a unified approach would be desirable. But at the same time there is too much shared ground to justify a claim that the chapters simply represent alternatives grounded in clearly differentiated academic disciplines – anthropology, sociology, semiotics, linguistics, media studies.

There is a rationale for the chapter sequence which has a loose but, we think, valid theoretical grounding in our assumptions about the shifting relations of text to context – discussed further on. Simplifying considerably, and using a terminology which none of us is particularly comfortable with, we can say that the movement is from the most 'textualist' to the most 'contextualist' of the five studies. That is to say, that whereas the first chapter begins by inviting the reader to think about the significance of single clauses in textualizing 'poverty', the final chapter takes us into a semiotics of everyday life for beggars and begged-from on the streets of London, where symbolic materials are developed and deployed, becoming then variously available for re-inscription, retextualization, within the secondary representations of the mass media corpus. The movement in the first chapter, by Gunther Kress, is from the single clause, to the bounded newspaper 'story' in which it occurs, to the layout of the page together with the other texts, verbal and visual, on which the story appears. In the second chapter, by Brian Street, we stay with the print medium, and a mainly text-based study, but this one ranges over the entire set of print stories concerned with poverty in Britain from our corpus. The third chapter, by Ulrike Meinhof, moves from the print medium to that of television, and interrogates the significance of a single documentary programme, in part by 'internal' investigation of its verbal and visual discourse, but also by reference to intertextual relations between that programme and another one, designed to be critical of the first. Chapter 4, by Kay Richardson, is concerned with this same programme, pursuing further the social meanings of 'poverty' by getting groups of viewers to talk about their reactions to this text. Finally, the fifth chapter, by Roger Hewitt, discusses the profoundly dialogic concepts and practices of 'poverty', drawing not only upon the mass media texts themselves, but also upon the audience data discussed in the preceding chapter, and upon observations of begging encounters in the capital city.

This brief description of what the book contains no doubt raises more questions than it answers. Later in this introduction we shall be offering more extended summaries of the individual chapters, as well as discussing in great depth some of the theoretical issues that are of concern to us all. Foremost among these issues is the theoretical validity of our structuring principle. Convenient though it is to adopt a metaphor of scale – texts of increasing 'size' – and an expansionary trajectory along that scale, with context given greater and greater 'weight' in the interpretations, the metaphor will mislead if it is forced into service as the basis of a theoretical model.

First, however, it is appropriate to indicate how we set about the project and the nature of the materials which we collected.

Poverty in Britain

At the end of the 1980s it seemed that poverty had returned to the political agenda in this country. The mass media began once again to talk about the 'poor', and to provide a forum for discussions about the existence of a poverty line. This made 'poverty' an eminently suitable choice of topic for our studies – highly controversial, highly 'mediated' and yet at the same time not remote from the experiential realities of those who would read and view the mediated accounts. In our media-rich society most citizens will have been exposed to parts of this poverty debate, and thus to representations of deprivation in Britain. The role of such representations – their production, interpretation, contestation – is increasingly recognized in the human sciences to be of crucial political importance. It is in part through such representations that we come to know what the world is like, and our 'lived realities' are scarcely independent of that media-derived knowledge.

The corpus

We said above that our project could be characterized principally as an attempt to develop and present a range of different methodological approaches to the analysis of discourse, to be pursued by focusing upon the discourses of poverty in the British mass media. So our aim was to investigate how a particularly important area of social life is mediated through the press and television, and to lay bare in our respective analyses the different approaches we used.

First of all we needed to find out which aspects of poverty or the poor in Britain are voiced through the media. What is deemed newsworthy – in view of the fact that absolute poverty, that is, the starvation, poverty-related sickness, and death of many millions of the world's population are competing for media coverage?

To answer this question we needed to collect a representative body of texts. The period we chose, in advance, for our survey, was from 24 April to 3 May 1991. The choice of these particular days was arbitrary, in the sense that we decided beforehand on a particular period so as not to predefine the discussion by any knowledge or expectations as to the kind of events that would trigger reporting about poverty during that time. We deliberately did not choose a specific key event from past years, and look for coverage of that single event across a range of media. We were more interested in the everyday, mundane coverage of poverty, even in the absence of any central trigger event. The advance decision to take a clearly defined period allowed us to survey a large section of the British press and television media. We hoped that this would make our sample as representative as possible. Once a pool of texts was thus established, we each opted for particular subsections of the material which struck us as most relevant to the theme of our book, the discussion about poverty in the British media, and which would also allow us to demonstrate our respective methods of analysis.

From the print media we surveyed the following titles:

Broadsheets: *The Guardian*, *The Independent*, *The Times*, and *The Daily Telegraph*
Tabloids: the *Daily Mail*, *The Sun*, the *Daily Express* and the *Evening Standard*
Sunday papers: *The Sunday Telegraph*, *The Sunday Times*, *The Independent on Sunday*, and *The Observer*
Journals: *Time Out*, *New Statesman*, *Economist* and *The Spectator*

Television search of that period produced one episode of the series *Breadline Britain*. In the evening TV news (Channel 4, 7.00 pm; BBC 1, 9.00 pm; ITN, 10.00 pm; BBC 2, Newsnight 10.30 pm) poverty in the UK was notably absent. This is due to the absence of any central 'trigger' event which would have put poverty on the national agenda. Without such an event, poverty is not news. It only appeared on the margins of reports about other items such as the reporting of a strike by the Liverpool binmen because of redundancy (*News at Ten*, 28 April), which showed houses in disrepair and rubbish-strewn streets. This was referred to by the commentary as a 'scene like Calcutta'. Only once in the same news broadcast were home repossessions through mortgage default mentioned. The newspapers can afford, for reasons of space, to be less parsimonious in their interpretation of 'news'.

In relation to the Third World, however, poverty was very much on the television agenda, a point discussed in Chapter 2. Poverty was discussed in relation to the plight of the Kurds in Iraq; in connection with the catastrophic effects of the cyclone in Bangladesh; as part of a discussion of a Christian Aid advertisement for famine relief similar in theme to the prominently reported speech by the Princess Royal for the Save the Children campaign, namely a contrast between the food consumed in the West and how the cost involved in buying even the smallest of items, for example, one bag of crisps, would help feed the starving in Africa. One of the longer features on Channel 4 discussed unemployment and poverty in the United States of America.

Forms and themes

The newspaper articles of our sample carried many more stories about the United Kingdom; they put poverty in the following typical contexts:

1. *Policy-related articles*: problems with the social services; unclaimed benefits, injustice in distribution of benefits (e.g. mortgage payments to wealthy unemployed); launch of new proposals (Labour Party) for family benefit.
2. *Poverty and health/welfare*: homelessness; squatters; poverty and drugs; violence on the streets (e.g. killings in Manchester's Moss Side district).
3. *'Human interest' stories*, such as stories about individuals involved in poverty-inspired theft or suicide.
4. *Stories about representation*: the NALGO poster/advertising campaign and the controversy it provoked.

As was to be expected, and irrespective of political tendencies, the tabloids differed from the broadsheets both in relation to the kind of story they were most likely to report, and, less obviously, in their style of reporting. These differences can best be described as a distinction between the private and the public sphere. Stories which were related to debates or changes in policy or public administration, which would affect in some ways the poorer sections of the British population – the unemployed, the unwell, single mothers, old age pensioners, and so on – regularly appeared, and produced comment, in the broadsheets, but were much less apparent in the tabloids during that period. Typical headlines were, for example, 'Ministers urged to compel jobless to work for benefits', *The Independent* 29 April; 'Child benefit tops Labour promises to aid families', *The Daily Telegraph*, 24 April; 'Poverty trap for lone mothers', *The Guardian*, 7 May. Unsurprisingly, the tabloid papers showed an overwhelming tendency to report stories from the other category of news stories, those which reported events in the private domain, witnessed by headlines such as 'Jobless Paul in suicide horror', *Daily Mirror*, 30 April; 'It's your life or your home', *Daily Mirror*, 3 May; 'School banishes boy too poor to pay for uniform', *Daily Express*, 3 May; 'Jail for loving mother who turned to robbery', *Daily Express*, 27 April. This polarity between describing structural changes in the organization of a particular society on the one hand, and narrating the actual concrete colourful instance of the fate of any one particular member of that society is one of the obvious dividing lines between the serious and the popular press in the representation of social reality through the print media.[1]

For a medium like television and its news and documentary broadcasting, this dividing line is much more difficult to establish, since by definition each image, each picture of a homeless person, or a patient waiting for an operation is simultaneously an instance of itself, and of something more general which it is intended to illustrate. It is thus idiosyncratic and representative at the same time. The problems this raises will be discussed in detail in Chapter 3.

After the pool of material was established amongst our research group, we selected specific texts for our respective chapters. The following media texts were followed up in one or more of the chapters of this book:

1. 'School banishes boy too poor to pay for uniform', *Daily Express*, 3 May (in Chapter 2).
2. The NALGO posters, and the press row about them (in Chapters 2, 3 and 5).
3. 'No place like home', programme 4 of *Breadline Britain* (in Chapters 3, 4 and 5).

'No place like home' was broadcast during our survey period, but we have made reference also to other episodes of the show broadcast outside that period, to press reactions to the series, and to one episode of *The Media Show*, also broadcast outside the survey period. This particular episode (from 16 March, Channel 4) critically discussed televisual representations of poverty, and focused in part on the making of *Breadline Britain* itself.

These texts form the core of our analysis of media representations of poverty in the UK. But each chapter frames those texts in relation to a discursive context that is relevant to that particular analysis. In doing so, each draws upon other textual materials, some of which were published/broadcast during our survey period and some which were not, but which have clearly marked intertextual relations with the core texts.

The chapters

Chapter 1

The book begins with a chapter by Gunther Kress which is the most micro-analytic of all the five substantive chapters in the volume. Its point of departure is a single text from our print corpus: 'School banishes boy too poor to pay for uniform', from the *Daily Express*, May 3 1991, by Ian McGregor, the Education Correspondent. The chapter begins with a discussion of the grammar of the single word 'poverty'. Then it opens out into the discussion of one key clause in the text: 'his parents could not afford a uniform'. From there it goes on to compare the grammar and semantics of that clause with others in the text, to demonstrate the existence of deep-seated and covert but systematic patterns of coding which, it is argued, correspond to specific and familiar ideologies in British culture concerning poverty. In one of these ideologies, expressed through a set of clauses, to be or to become poor is to be in a condition for which you bear no personal responsibility. Poverty is not done by its sufferer, nor is it done to the sufferer – it is not an action or event at all but a state. Yet there is another ideology which corresponds to other clauses and to divergent readings of the same clauses as in the previous set, which is compatible with the more reactionary ideology in which the poor are responsible for their own poverty. The fact that the same clauses (under different interpretations) can feature within different ideologies is rhetorically functional here, for this is a newspaper which while it might wish to advance a reactionary line (and indeed in editorial columns routinely does so quite explicitly) would for reasons of circulation not wish to foreclose on the alternative to such a degree as to alienate readers more sympathetic to the latter. Hence, a textual ambivalence is the result, rather than 'objectivity' or 'lack of bias'.

With this particularly story, which is not only about poverty but also about the politics of education, the hardship suffered by the schoolboy victim (and his parents therefore) allows for an analysis in terms of responsibility which neither makes the family unambiguously responsible for their own distress, nor treats that distress as a state of affairs beyond the scope of human agency. As Gunther Kress explains it, the clauses of the text are so organized as to express through their attributions of agenthood a very definite if covert explanation concerning the question of responsibility in this instance. Not surprisingly, responsibility is attributed to those very social actors whom the Conservative Right so disparages, the components of the educational establishment at every level upwards from the individual schoolteacher to the local council. The individual confronts the system and is oppressed by it.

Chapter 2

Chapter 2, by Brian Street, like the one before it, focuses upon the press material from our original corpus. But for Brian Street the relevant context for assessing the significance of those texts is at a different level than for Gunther Kress. Here we see the stories about poverty in Britain framed in relation to stories of poverty and hardship abroad. During the period of our survey, the British mass media, in its international coverage, included much news and many images from the Third World. Notwithstanding the formal separation of international from national news and features, the co-presence of the national and the international discourse sets up for readers and viewers intertextual relations between the two. In one domain, the domain of Third World wars and catastrophes, poverty can be equated with the extremes of human suffering where survival itself is the issue. The other domain, that of British poverty, gives rise to talk about the quality of life that is apparently far removed from survival. To make a connection between these domains is to conclude, maybe, that the latter concerns are trivial and indulgent ones by comparison with the trials of the Kurds, Ethiopians, Bangladeshis, and so on. Where the British 'poverty discourse' is dominated by a fairly academic and technical argument about the appropriate way of determining the poverty threshold, the international frame is, both in images and in words, more directly emotionally resonant. Where the Third World poor (the Kurds, notably) are oppressed by a malevolent dictator, the British state by contrast can only seem benign. Where the Third World is inhabited by victims and supplicants, the inhabitants of the First World are to the former the saviours and providers. Visual images, needless to say, are of the essence in permitting such contrastive inferences to be drawn. Brian Street notes that the international stories produced a considerable amount of photo-journalism in the press, in which use was made of a particular 'stock image' – that of the mother with suckling infant, closely related to the Madonna and Child of Western iconography. But the starving Third World mother cannot nourish her child in this fashion, for she herself is so close to starvation: without milk but still posed in the madonna suckling position, she becomes a new icon for poverty, calling upon those earlier Christian themes and metonymically linking the issues of poverty in the Third World and in the West.

Chapter 3

Chapter 3 by Ulrike Meinhof, moves the book from the print media to television. It is principally concerned to present a social semiotic analysis of the television series *Breadline Britain*, with especial reference to episodes one and four of that series. Episode four was broadcast during our survey period. Since Meinhof's socio-semiotic approach encourages an interest in alternative representations of particular aspects of social reality, and in contestation between accounts, the chapter is also concerned with the substance and form of one episode of *The Media Show*, a Channel 4 series which takes a critical view of the media industries and media practices. The episode concerned was itself focused upon the question of the televisual representation of poverty, and in that context *Breadline Britain* specifically came in for critical attention.

The semiotic analysis of *Breadline Britain* is concerned to explore the contributions of the verbal discourse, the images and the music to the significance of the programme as a whole. A principal question for this analysis is the programme's overt reliance upon a discourse of expertise – specifically the discourse of social science. The programme derives from a quantitative study of the British population which was specifically conducted to find out where, for our society, consensus would place the poverty line. Relative to that consensual definition of the nature of poverty in the UK, the number and proportion of people in the country who are poor were established. The televisualization of these academic propositions is a challenging task and one which the programme confronts by trying to make the visual imagery subordinate to the verbal discourse in which the academic project is explained. Written text on screen is also used in this attempt to tell the viewers what, for *Breadline Britain*, is going to count as poverty and why. Then, the specific households which function as the programme's case studies of poverty throughout the series, are selected on the basis of their relation to specific categories of poverty determined by the academic research. Particularly in the first episode the camera is asked to bear direct and concurrent witness to statements about personal circumstances as made by the subjects themselves on the programme. Yet there is more to the semiosis of *Breadline Britain* than a straightforward encoding of verbal statements into corresponding literal pictures. Specifically, and this is where the analysis of the music becomes significant too, the programme constructs for its viewers a mood of melancholia. It is possible to see *Breadline Britain* as a programme trying, rhetorically, to 'play safe'. Not only does it try to establish and work from a consensual definition of poverty, it also seeks to avoid any of the imagery that depicts a less submissive face of poverty – joy-riding, theft, drug-taking, tense and aggressive scenes with institutional representatives, and the like. For *Breadline Britain*'s poor are without exception the deserving poor.

When it comes to contrasting *Breadline Britain* with *The Media Show*, the point here is to expose aspects of the latter's critique as simplistic accounts of the nature of representation. *Breadline Britain*, claims *The Media Show*, has in effect 'lied' about the poor in Britain because some of the people featured in particular shots were ony displaying (i.e. acting) the behaviour that the shots represented. On that particular day when the cameras were in town these people did not sleep on the streets. While the circumstances of this 'fake' for Meinhof make the charge of falsification a misplaced one, her principal concern is not so much to defend *Breadline Britain* within these parameters of truth and falsehood, but to demonstrate that *The Media Show* itself can do no more than present viewers with a construction of 'reality'. They, too, must provide a context for the speech and behaviour of their subjects which is no less a construction than the one in *Breadline Britain*, albeit a different construction and one positioned to challenge it.

Chapter 4

Chapter 4, by Kay Richardson, is an attempt to extend our collective investigation of the meaning of poverty in the British news media by moving the interpretative focus away from the texts themselves and on to the interaction between texts and their viewers; it starts from the premise that meaning does not reside 'in' a text to be passively recorded by the text's recipients. Rather, it is only when recipients engage with the text using their own frameworks of interpretation, cultural knowledge and value systems that meaning is produced. Both of the chapters before this one took specific texts as their point of departure. Chapter 4 does likewise; indeed it is a vital counterpart to Chapter 3, Ulrike Meinhof's account of *Breadline Britain*, and in particular to the account in that chapter of the fourth episode, 'No place like home'. This episode was screened to selected groups of viewers who were subsequently invited to discuss their reactions to it. Not unexpectedly there was both sympathy and lack of sympathy among the viewer groups. The sympathetic groups in a sense had an easier time of it, for they perceived that the programme was sympathetic too, which meant that there was a kind of alignment at the level of evaluation. More unsympathetic groups had to find ways of dealing with the depictions that made sense of the sympathy ingredient (analysed in this chapter as grounded in a liberal discourse on poverty) without committing them to sharing it. This could, for example, take the form of accepting that the case histories of Chapter 4 (homeless Kim, Alison in a bed and breakfast hotel, Yvonne in a substandard council flat) were deserving but unrepresentative, thus resisting or, rather, overriding the (implicit) claim to typicality upon which the case history approach depends. In some cases too, perceiving their own lack of sympathy to be out of line with what the programme expects from them, viewers (notably the Townswomen's Guild panels) would express anxiety that they were the 'wrong people' to be watching the programme in the first place, and thus the 'wrong people' even to be participating in the audience research. This mismatch they would attribute to their generation principally, their experiences of poverty in the 1930s having been a powerful influence in determining the value systems through which they continued to live their lives and understand the world. Roger Hewitt in Chapter 5 offers a somewhat different explanation of their reaction, attributing it more to social class than to generational difference between these viewers and the programme-makers.

But sympathizers did not simply fall into step with the programme's own rhetoric. On the contrary, some felt that the programme misrepresented the true extent of poverty by not concentrating upon extreme cases: others, accepting the point that these were not extreme cases then defended the programme following more or less its own principle that extreme, absolute deprivation is an unjust criterion of poverty in a world where living standards for the majority are rising.

Despite this degree of variation in the responses to *Breadline Britain* it did seem that there was a substantial amount of convergence in what the viewers thought the text was saying. Thus by and large they all thought that the programme was sympathetic even when themselves resisting or questioning that degree of sympathy.

Chapter 5

Chapter 5 by Roger Hewitt attempts to establish connections between, on the one hand, the representation and conduct of poverty on the streets, and on the other hand its second-order, mass media representation. Poverty is not now, nor has it ever been, just a matter of material existence for poor people. It is, too, a symbolic state, a state that must be appropriately embodied in its representatives. The bodies and accoutrements of the poor must bear direct, 'true' witness to their poverty – just as much on the streets as on television or in the press. And the appropriate signifiers of poverty are signifiers devoid of connotative meanings beyond the domains where poverty stakes a claim. Connotations of dirt and ill-health are acceptable, for poverty can encompass these manifestations. Connotations of aesthetic value are unacceptable – as are signifiers which speak of pleasure rather than survival, choice rather than necessity.

The street poor – those who, jobless and homeless, resort to begging in order to survive – come closer than most in this country to poverty's ideal representatives (though as Brian Street argues in his chapter, victims of Third World wars and disasters are probably even closer to that ideal), for they have little more than their bodies with which to accomplish the semiotic task. Thus the semiotic measure of poverty bears a truly stark character: and individual failures to come up to the mark are triggers for public scepticism, whatever the substance or context of the particular case, on the street or in the mass media. Beggars in Britain may, in construing themselves relative to this semiotic benchmark, understand that they are not yet 'the poor', for all that they are adopting the strategies of poverty.

In the public, political argument about poverty, iconographic and semiotic concerns are often subordinated to substantive ones, though it is not possible either to exclude the former nor entirely to separate them from the latter. Often they are contextualized within a discourse concerned with the bureaucratic management of poverty – that is to say, with questions of public policy regarding the terms and conditions of state provision for the poor. *Breadline Britain* (discussed in Ulrike Meinhof's chapter) deploys this discourse in resisting as it does the official criteria for determining the poverty threshold and working out its own. It also constructs its own categories of poor experience, providing accounts of hardship and obstacles to overcoming it from within these categories.

And here it confronts several dimensions of public scepticism: one is concerned with the claim of the poor upon the rest of society; another – a form of semiotic scepticism – with whether you can believe what you see; a further with other motivations in the representation game. Viewers can speculate, for example, about why middle-class professionals working in television, themselves remote from the experience of poverty, might have an interest in promoting one view of the poor rather than another. Further, the bureaucratic management discourse can be resisted, challenged, or can simply fail to engage subjects whose experiences or social class position, or perhaps both, keep them at a distance from its mode of understanding. Roger Hewitt re-examines viewers' reactions to *Breadline Britain* (i.e. the material examined by Kay Richardson in Chapter 4) and demonstrates the existence of an alternative to this bureaucratic discourse, one concerned with the personal management of poverty. From the perspective of this discourse, *Breadline Britain* can seem highly unsatisfactory to an ex-street person who knows so much more than the programme does about the lived experience of poverty. But it can, too, seem unsatisfactory to senior citizens remembering the 1930s who object to the lack of 'spirit' in the modern poor, their expectation of finding help from the agencies of the welfare state, rather than pursuing their own salvation from poverty. The case histories in *Breadline Britain* are taken by such viewers to exemplify this spinelessness.

Discourse and cultural 'reading'

Earlier we defined our joint enterprise as one that was concerned with the nature of social meaning, its production and reproduction, principally as this works through the conduit of mass media texts. The theorization of 'the text', of textuality and intertextuality is, of course, much debated in linguistics, literary and cultural studies (see, e.g., Frow 1986; Hodge 1990; Jameson 1991; Rosenau 1992) though this is not the place for an overview or critique of these bodies of work. Suffice it to say that our own work shares in that 'textualist' emphasis which is now part of so much sociocultural research – research in which a Foucaultian notion of 'discourse' is an informing and organizing concept (Foucault 1970a and b).

It is not always clear what theoretical and methodological issues hang on the choice of the term 'discourse' as against the term 'ideology' to refer to a more or less systematic framework of understanding that permits the expression or 'realization' of particular meanings in textual forms. It is not always clear whether the underlying theoretical framework is one that requires both terms, with conceptually distinct significance. The history of the latter term, 'ideology', locates it within Marxist academic scholarship, though it was never confined within explicitly Marxist work; the term 'discourse' bears fewer traces of a Marxist heritage. Then, the term 'discourse' emphasizes more a specifically linguistic character to the phenomenon it indexes than does the term 'ideology'. In the chapters which follow this introduction, both terms are used. Gunther Kress, more than the other authors, talks in terms of specific ideologies concerning the nature of poverty. This is in keeping with the tradition of critical linguistics with which he is associated, and which, in part, his chapter here represents. Other chapters identify, for example, liberal and conservative discourses on poverty (see Chapter 4); a discourse concerned with the bureaucratic management of poverty and one concerned with the personal management of poverty (see Chapter 5).

What we want to do now is to highlight a few of the conceptual issues which arise in trying to 'read' cultural texts in relation to their discursive origins, and discuss further the concept of discourse as it is now commonly used in non-positivist social research. The most important issues which emerged for us were, first, the scope for interpretative variation of any given text, genre or corpus; secondly, the limits of the conventional view of a text as a bounded object, to be interpreted within a given or negotiated context; and thirdly, the relation of texts to extra-textual 'reality'. Clearly, these issues are interrelated; separating them may be a somewhat artificial exercise, but helps nevertheless to clarify the problems involved in undertaking this kind of cultural and textual analysis. If the discussions which follow seem somewhat inconclusive, this reflects the fact that our different approaches and understandings have not yet resolved themselves into a single framework that we all share.

The very ideal of 'a text' invites a misleadingly objectivist view, not just of supra-sentential linguistic form, but also, and much more damagingly, of supra-sentential meaning. Texts are not objects, like chairs and tables, even if the language we use for talking about them betrays us into thinking of them as such. 'Text' as a mass rather than a count noun points us in the right kind of direction. There are of course linguistic practices which themselves collude with the objectivist view – notably, for our purposes, the practice of realizing news discourse in newspapers as blocks of words, visually separated from similar blocks by white space and lines. The alternative, 'interpretivist' view of textual meaning insists, first, on the importance of recognizing the readerly competences which bear down upon the production of meaning from text. Secondly, it insists upon the importance of the social and discursive context within which 'the text' occurs.

Interpretative variation

Scholarly, 'expert', critical readings are nothing new in media and cultural studies research. But such readings are easy to challenge – their status in relation to 'lay' readings is often unclear, and thus they lack authority. Ordinary newspaper readers and television viewers are not looking for ideological meanings, and may reject such interpretations when presented with them. A psycho-analytical reading will make different claims from a more sociocultural one, and the appeals to different epistemological frameworks will render invalid any attempt to adjudicate between those readings. One response to this relativist impasse has been to shift the focus from the readings of the textual experts to those of 'real' readers and viewers. Critics and analysts of this persuasion no longer read texts; they read readings. Chapter 4 below comes out of this tradition. Richardson in that chapter claims: 'It is one thing to present a textual analysis of a television programme or any other kind of mass media text. It is a different matter to say whether and how far the meanings which the analyst attributes to the programme are the "realized meanings" so far as the viewers are concerned' (p. 93). It is important to be clear, though, where this interest in realized meanings can lead, and to give some thought to the consequences of shifting attention from texts to readers (or viewers) of texts.

Theoretically speaking this shift of attention can lead to a position in which analysts' readings are simply deemed illegitimate – or, at best, seen as a kind of self-examination, of no broader social significance. None of the writers contributing to the present volume has gone down that particular cul-de-sac. It represents a degree of solipsism and radical scepticism concerning what can be known that, I think, we all reject, though possibly for different reasons. Even the 'audience study' chapter itself was predicated upon the analytic study of *Breadline Britain* provided in Chapter 3. Furthermore, though it asks questions about the degree of interpretative variation as between the various groups who viewed 'No place like home' and discussed it, the chapter ends with a conclusion stressing a substantial amount of interpretative convergence among the viewing groups. There is an interesting complementarity between Chapter 4 and Chapter 1. We have presented Chapter 1, by Gunther Kress, as the most 'textualist' of all the studies. Here, then, is where our readers might expect the greatest degree of commitment to a view of the text as a self-contained object. But that is a view which Kress explicitly rejects, despite offering the tightest kind of textual microanalysis. His claim is that the microanalysis can itself provide evidence for two or three distinct groups of readers, ideologically speaking, each of which would be cued in to determinately different meanings through different but equally 'real' clause patterns. Of course it remains an open question whether the readers do in fact align themselves with these textually available reading positions, and this is where empirical research with the consumers of newspapers would come in. But the absence here of a complementary study of readings need not invalidate the textual approach.

The displacement of textual approaches in media studies comes about in part as a reaction against pessimistic and negative views of the audience in an earlier phase of research, depicting readers and viewers principally as victims, without any power to resist the ideological messages conveyed in and through media texts. Yes, readers and viewers make meaning. But they do not do so free of interpretative constraints that are part of their own histories, shaped by their encounters with previous texts and genres. 'Depth interpretation', then, takes a certain amount for granted concerning the nature of those constraints, and is open to challenge when the assumptions made do not ring true. But it would be intellectually inhibiting to build scepticism into the procedures to such an extent as to prohibit researchers from making any assumptions about the kinds of things that viewers and readers already know, either at the level of their linguistic competences or of a more substantive kind.

Text and context: shifting boundaries

The 'meaning' produced from text is determined in part by the contextual frame within which the text is placed. The same sentence may be given a different reading according to whether it appears in a *Daily Mirror* (labourist left-wing) or a *Daily Express* (right-wing) news report. But there are undoubtedly problems in applying this view of textual meaning in practical analysis, not least because the concept of 'context' itself has such a wide range of meanings. 'Context' can mean anything from global social structure, to immediate social situation, to co-text – and can incorporate, too, the readers' contributions to the sense-making process, their discursive competences and evaluative frameworks. It would appear that text/context boundaries are not objectively given, but as with other aspects of textual meaning, are established and negotiated in and through the process of sense-making. We are learning to understand the text/context boundary as something which is variable, unstable, and operative at different levels. This formulation may make it sound impossibly open-ended and indeterminate. In practice, this principle of shifting boundaries is operationalized in fairly specific ways, which are available therefore for critical appraisal.

Thus for example in Chapter 1, Gunther Kress asks us to consider what interpretative difference it makes if, instead of looking for covert explanations of poverty within the frame of a single article, which acts as the context-of-interpretation for the constituent clauses, we 'reframe' at the level of the page. The motivation for this reframing is partially a question of production strategy. The page has been designed in the newspaper offices as a complete unit. It is also in part a question of readerly strategy – readers confronting the page 'as a whole' may or may not read across as well as within items, with different effects depending upon the dimension of time in their reading practice – where they start and the order in which items are read. At this level, the page is the context-of-interpretation for the items within it. From the analyst's point of view this move entails a loss of determinacy. We can be much less sure of what readers other than ourselves actually do at this level. But the theoretical point is an important one, and it is valuable to demonstrate what possibilities exist so that these can be tested 'in the field'. The dimension of time is not 'wired in' at page level in anything like as firm a way as it is with the single news story produced according to the convention that makes us read sentences in a particular order. Analytically speaking, this may tempt us to abstract away from the time dimension in our subsequent analytic reading: story A bears upon the meaning of story B, story B bears upon that of story A; since we can privilege neither of these relationships, there is a larger 'meaning' consisting of both stories 'together', which is now simultaneously in time, after the consecutive possibilities have been allowed for – or indeed, instead of the consecutive possibilities. Whether we should give in to this temptation is an important question. Will it depend upon whether or not we think that real readers make this abstracting move?

This is a question in which the question of interpretative strategies and the question of text/context boundaries are linked. But even if we remain at the level of the primary text, the story not the page, the question of part-whole relations needs to be conceptualized in relation to readerly (viewerly) strategies. Cognitive approaches to discourse comprehension have long explained the processes of understanding texts as an interplay of essentially two central types of comprehension strategies: top-down or concept-driven and bottom-up or data-driven strategies (van Dijk and Kintsch 1983). Corner (1991) contains a related discussion of the 'part-whole' problem from the perspective of the viewer – he is thinking principally of television. He points out that although viewers do collect meanings incrementally from the parts of texts and work outwards to the meaning of the whole, they also pre-empt the conclusion of that enterprise, anticipate the meaning of the whole and use that global interpretation in assigning meanings at the micro level. This 'looping' between the micro and the macro may or may not be relevant to newspaper forms at *page* level. Corner also distinguishes this size-of-text 'loop' from a parallel one concerned with the level of meaning, distinguishing between denotation, connotation and significance. With the first we can talk of simple comprehension; with the second, of apprehending associative meaning. The third he defines as:

a level at which viewers and readers attach a generalised significance to what they have seen and heard, evaluating it (perhaps in relation to its perceived presuppositions and entailments if it has propositional force) and locating it within a negotiated place in their knowledge or memory, where it may continue to do modifying work on other constituents of their consciousness (and, indeed, of their unconscious) (Corner 1991: 272).

This 'linearity' loop involves anticipations of global significance which permit particular sentences and images to be heard or seen as having congruent denotation and connotation, even while denotations and connotations themselves act as triggers in allowing significance to be projected.

One way to conceive of interpretative relations between items on the same page might be via the idea of intertextuality. With the time dimension removed, the different articles on the same page can be seen as intertexts for one another – not, in this case, because of overt intertextual reference, but because of the way their meanings impinge upon one another. There is of course the formal context itself – the composited page – which encourages? invites? allows? that interplay. What happens to intertextuality in the absence of such a formal frame? Chapters 2 and 3 provoke the asking of this question – though in different ways. Meinhof is confronting two texts, *Breadline Britain* and *The Media Show* where one-way intertextual reference is explicit. The latter text knew about the existence of the former and made reference to it. Brian Street is producing an argument in which, according to him, it makes a difference to the meaning of stories about domestic poverty when these are read in a context which includes the international hardship stories. The 'frame' used by Street in producing this analysis is at a higher level again – that of the print corpus as a whole, and with some reference, too, to concurrent television news imagery. In one sense this move takes us away from the focus upon readerly experience as the basis of the analyst's interpretative authority – the idea that the analyst is doing, in an explicit way, what (some) real readers may have done unconsciously. For there can be few if any 'real' readers who, during the period in question, 'experienced' all of the textual material that Street examined in producing his account, and it would be ridiculous to make this criterial in assessing the value of that account. But since there is an implicit quantitative dimension to Street's study, that is, a focus upon the range and amount of material available during the period in question, it only needs to be plausible that British people have seen enough of that sort of thing, to make it likewise plausible that the connections Street makes are realized in the heads of the readers and viewers.

It is this reliance in Street's chapter upon the range and amount of relevant story types in the print corpus that begins to point in the direction of discourse in the Foucaultian sense as the relevant contextual frame for analytic interpretation. Discourse, for Street, is yet another level of context, 'above' the sentence, 'above' the text, 'above' the page. The spatial metaphor begins to strain at this point, and with good reason.

If discourses are socially grounded interpretative frameworks, based in specific social institutions, they can be seen to act, within those institutions, as powerful forms of knowledge which structure and constrain what can be thought, said and done by social actors. To study the social order is then, in part, to study discursive relations – convergences and divergences within and between them, their degrees of robustness under challenge, their scope of application, the emotional and moral investments that subjects make in particular discourses, the interests they serve, and so on.

Texts, then, can be viewed as generically conditioned expressions or realizations of such discursive formations. Here we can see one reason why a one-dimensional spatial metaphor breaks down when we try to treat discourse as another level of context. Up to this point the spatial metaphor worked because text/context boundaries could, more or less, all be conceived on the same plane of realization – even if we allowed that realization to depend upon viewers'/readers' interpretative strategies. Now we are trying to think in terms of text/context boundaries that cross over from the plane of realization to the plane of formations.

Brian Street's chapter can in fact be seen as itself enacting that movement across the planes. Above we suggested that the range and amount of particular story types in the press corpus were relevant to the validity of his analysis in which the international, Third World stories are seen to provide an interpretative context for stories of domestic poverty. To say that is already to begin to block out the 'context' in terms of its underlying discourses. Street as the analyst recognizes or hypothesizes the relevant categories for this blocking out because of his familiarity with their typical motifs, images, idioms, themes and so on.

An over-elaborate theoreticist topography of text-context relations is something we very much want to avoid producing, even if the language of the foregoing suggests an implicit topographical model. More worthwhile than following up the implications of the levels-and-planes schema in that way, is considering where this perspective leaves the viewer/reader. We want to understand subjects, interpreting texts, as themselves possessing/possessed by, discursive repertoires. Furthermore, we want to find out what we can about the character of those discursive repertoires, their potential distribution amongst the population and the ways in which they are in fact activated in the processes of interpretation. Chapters 4 and 5 move out in that direction. Richardson and Hewitt, in their different ways, both attempt to use other sorts of data, 'outside' what the mass media have to offer, in order to explore what it is that readers and viewers already understand – and what becomes of those understandings in the encounter with the media text.

Notes

1. That last story, of a woman convicted of robbing Building Societies, also appeared in the broadsheets, variously labelling the protagonist 'woman', 'devoted wife', 'mother'. The headlines included: 'Devoted wife turned robber to pay the bills', *The Daily Telegraph*, 27 April; 'Woman who caught bus to rob building societies is jailed', *The Times*, 27 April.

References

Corner, J. (1991) Meaning, genre, and context: the problematics of 'public knowledge' in the new audience studies. In Curran, J. (ed.) *Mass Media and Society*. London: Arnold.

Foucault, M. (1970a) 'Ordre du Discours', Leçon Inaugurale au College de 1 et 2 Decembre 1970. Paris: Gallimard 1971. Trans. 'The Order of Discourse'. In Young, Robert (ed.) *Untying the Text* (1981). London: Routledge & Kegan Paul.

Foucault, M. (1970b) *The Order of Things*. London: Tavistock.

Frow, J. (1986) *Marxism and Literary History*. Oxford: Blackwell.

Hodge, R. (1990), *Literature as Discourse*. Cambridge: Polity Press.

Jameson, F. (1991) *Postmodernism, or the Cultural Logic of Late Capitalism*. London: Verso.

Rosenau, P. M. (1992) *Post-Modernism and the Social Sciences*. Princeton: Princeton University Press.

Van Dijk, T. A. and Kintsch, W. (1983) *Strategies of Discourse Comprehension*. London: Academic Press.

1 *Text and grammar as explanation*

Gunther Kress

The task of the media is to make sense of the world for their audiences. That 'making of sense' involves providing explanations. These come in many forms. There is the explanation involved in the selection of events. This explanation consists in saying: 'These are the events to attend to'; and, by implication 'don't bother yourself with the rest'. The selected events have to be 'mediated', and this involves a second, a different kind of explanation. It consists in saying: 'That's what this event is like, and that's how it is best understood.'

Both kinds of explanation, through selection and through mediation, arise in particular social structures and histories, and necessarily make use of particular modes and media of representation. The social structures and histories on the one hand, and the modes and media of representation on the other, have decisive effects on the form which these explanations take. The former shape and affect largely *what* is mediated – what issues are dealt with, what aspects of these issues are made focal, and what explanatory accounts are provided. The latter shape and affect how these issues can be and are mediated – what means and structures of representation are available, who are the audiences, what are the conditions of reception, and so on. Both must be attended to equally, for both are replete with social meanings. Both affect the shape of the text; for instance, the kind of issue that is focused on will have an effect, among many others, on the generic form of text chosen for its representation. The mode of representation will have an effect, among other things, on the reality status of the representation: the visual, for instance, being the more realistic medium compared to, say, language; and photographs being more realistic than drawings.

In this chapter I deal with the representation of poverty on one page of a tabloid newspaper. My reason for taking a whole page rather than just one – the most obviously relevant – article, is to make a number of points of a methodological and theoretical kind. For instance, I want to show that texts must always be read in the context of surrounding texts, and this theoretical/methodological point itself underlines the fact that explanations in the media are always set in a complex of other simultaneously given explanations, which together provide a more complex and yet also a more insistently pressing set of explanations. My account remains, nevertheless, a relatively simple one. That is not an indication of my sense that I have completed my task of explanation, but rather an indication of the fact that no explanatory or descriptive account is ever complete.

In dealing with a whole page the first question is 'Where do I start?' While those concerned with laying out a page of a newspaper have a quite clear sense of the structure of 'the whole page as a text', and of how it is to be read, readers develop their own ways of reading newspaper pages, or anything else for that matter, ways of reading which coincide to a greater or lesser extent with the intentions behind the layout of a paper (all Fig. 1.1). So in relation to this page some readers may prefer to focus on the images first; others may be drawn by the bold headline of the main article; a few may be interested in the advertisement. Some readers may follow a reading path which goes from the left of the page, broadly, to the right, which, in this case would mean focusing on the 'photonews' story first, and then on the main article (if that's what it is). The practices of readers are not accidents – 'we all just read in our own way' – but are shaped by a reader's social and cultural history.

My own reading, as a matter of record, followed a 'reading path' from the bold headline, to the initial paragraphs of the report; then to the images in the 'photo-news' section; later to the brief story within that ('A royal thank you . . .'); then to the advertisement; and only much later to the story, 'Car boss's plea . . .' and 'Earlobe risk'. However, my reading was strongly guided by the fact that I was about to do an analysis of this page.

Figure 1.1 Page reproduced from the *Daily Express*, Friday May 3 1991

Without that motivation I would probably not have paid much attention to the 'photonews' story (both because I dislike images of the 'private lives' of people in the media, and because I do not engage with 'stories' involving royalty); and I certainly would not have attempted to read the advertisement. As someone in the age category of those who feel increasingly nervous about various diseases I might have read the short report on 'Earlobe risk'.

The significance of an interest in the reading path is that on the one hand it reveals the reader's *interest*, which will shape the reading produced by any one reader, and, on the other hand, it matters whether I focus first on the photonews report and treat the 'School banishes boy' report as constituting its context, or vice-versa. In the former case I start with a focus on the caring state, and the 'School banishes boy' report shows that there are still some aspects of the institutional structures of the state which need fixing. In the latter case I start with a focus on the problems of poverty and its causes (and effects), and the photonews report shows that things could and should be otherwise. Also, and this is a third point in relation to reading paths, habitual ways of reading will make possible more or less resistant readings in relation to particular texts and particular media. For instance, my preference for printed language over visual images *in this context* makes me a less ready recipient for the message of the photonews report.

The kind of explanation which I am interested to describe in this chapter may itself need some description. The report on the banished child provides, on the face of it, its own explanatory account: a child has poor parents; they do not have sufficient money to buy a school uniform; bureaucrats who should assist are unwilling to do so; and his (uncaring?) school does not permit him to participate in normal classroom activity. That seems to be it. My interest extends beyond this explanation to a critical reading: in this complex of events I am interested to know how my reading is being structured, for instance, what kinds of actions are performed by what kinds of actors? What kinds of causes are identified? What kinds of causal connections are established? To get an answer to these questions I engage in some syntactic analysis, for grammar and syntax provide *their* particular explanations, which often differ from or add to those accessible to a more casual reading. In my critical reading I am also interested, for instance, to see what kinds of generic forms are used to construct explanations. The generic form 'report' is in itself an explanation, namely one that tells us about the status of the text: it *reports* what has happened; it is factual. But is a report the most apt form to provide a causal explanation? And if not, why is it used here? Beyond that, I am interested to note that apart from this one, possibly central, account of hardship there are others: as in the photonews story; or the hardship suffered by employers unable to afford company cars for their employees; or the potential hardship of those with earlobes of a particular shape. The fact that most, or all, of this page is given over to accounts of hardship of one kind or another suggests a more far-reaching explanation of poverty, one not provided by the single report on the banished school child, and not available by a focus on this single text outside the context of all texts on this page.

Hence a detailed analysis of all formal, textual and compositional aspects of this page is needed to reveal the more complex, and perhaps more covert explanations of the concept of poverty which this paper provides for its readers. It is also likely to reveal that any one newspaper is unlikely to have a single homogeneous account of an ideologically, socially and politically complex and difficult term such as poverty.

In this chapter I will first provide a partial syntactic analysis of the text which I take to be the focal text, the 'School banishes boy' text; I will then provide briefer analyses of the other texts on this page, and proceed from there to give a description of the 'grammar' of the whole page. From this I will construct an account of this paper's explanation of poverty. My intention is twofold: to establish a methodology of reading, and to uncover a particular explanation of poverty, a troubling social and ideological phenomenon for all sections of society, even if troubling in very different ways.

The grammar of poverty: the central text

Words bear the traces of their social histories of use. To enquire into the meaning of a word is to enquire into present attitudes and practices; it is also, in part at least, to uncover explanations. This applies equally to what we regard, broadly, as the 'meaning' of words, and to the grammar of words. The latter condenses histories of past associations, which found their expression in past syntactic associations and collocations, and descriptions of relations between objects and processes which a social group has found plausible and apt. The grammar of the noun 'poverty' may serve as an example. Poverty is something that you are *in*; this makes it unlike measles, for instance, or luck or hunger, which are things you can *have*. The place you are *in* when you are in poverty is an abstract place, like despair (which you are also *in*), a kind of mental place, an emotional state of affairs. Poverty is not active; it is something with which you are afflicted, like hunger. Poverty is a state; not an event. To say 'I am (living) in poverty' is to say 'I am poor'. It is a quality, a characteristic which acts as a description of a person, a classification.

This grammar is at once an explanation – not an overt, explicit explanation, but one which, being covert, is all the more potent in its effects. It tells us that poverty is something that you can be in, or get yourself into; that it is a classification of the person to whom it attaches: 'I am poor' is like 'I am tall' in that respect. The linguist Benjamin Lee Whorf pointed out that in English the order of adjectives in front of the noun indicated the degree to which a quality is regarded as intrinsic to the object named by the noun: the further from the noun the adjective, the less intrinsic the quality. In English we say 'those beautiful red shoes' rather than those 'red beautiful shoes', indicating that 'red' is regarded as being more intrinsic to those shoes than is 'beautiful'. Similarly we would say 'that tall poor man' more readily than we would say 'that poor tall man' (unless we used 'poor' in the meaning of pitiful, pathetic: 'what a pitiable tall man'). To be poor, it seems, is more intrinsic a property of humans than to be tall, at least that is, as far as the grammar of English is concerned.

How do you get to be poor, or to be in poverty, grammatically? Accidentally, it seems, as far as the grammar of English is concerned. We fall into poverty, find ourselves in poverty, become poor. It is not a state of being or a quality under our control. We don't move into poverty, nor do we acquire it (unlike the measles, which we 'get'). In other words, the grammar of poverty is not an agentive one; it is not the result of an action done deliberately by us in order to achieve that state. Poverty itself can, however, act agentively – poverty can drive us into despair, poverty causes the break up of families, and so on, as the media tell us every day.

Given this as the grammar of poverty, how does this fit with certain current ideologies which are its direct opposite? That is, how can you express the notion that the poor are responsible for their own poverty given that the grammar of English seems not to lend itself, easily, to such an account? That is the question I want to explore in relation to this article in the newspaper, the conservative *Daily Express*, from 3 May 1991.

School banishes boy too poor to pay for uniform

by Ian MacGregor

Education Correspondent

1. A SCHOOLBOY was taught in a class on his own because his parents could not afford a uniform, it was revealed yesterday.
2. The 13-year-old was separated from classmates for several weeks, a community advice organisation said.
3. His misery only ended when friends found enough jumble in an Oxfam shop for make-shift uniform.
4. 'It is the worst case of this kind we have seen', said Nichola Simpson, head of policy at the National Association of Citizens Advice Bureaux.
5. 'It was very distressing for a boy so young.
    (6) And he missed out educationally.
    (7) Children should not suffer like that, especially because they cannot afford a uniform.
    (8) It was a very hard-hearted thing to do.'
9. The incident happened in the East Midlands earlier this year when the boy's family moved into the area.
10. His parents were on income support, but education chiefs told them they did not qualify for a grant because their son moved schools mid-term.
11. The case was revealed by the association in a report on uniforms.
12. It said many poor children were suffering at school because local bureaucrats are not helping them pay for uniforms.
13. Many parents on benefits or low incomes were not receiving grants, which are discretionary.

DISCIPLINE

14. The news comes as many schools return to uniforms in a bid to make pupils more presentable and disciplined.
15. But the NACAB found local authority provision for uniform and clothing grants was tending to 'wither away'.
16. Assistant director Peter Hildrew added that grants were now a local priority for many education authorities.

17. 'Parents are penalised according to where they live', he said.
(18) The system is often arbitrary and seems close to collapse.

(Daily Express, 3.5.91)

Poverty is what the article is about; being poor to an extent that prohibits you from achieving a certain thing, namely paying for a uniform. The clause which initially caught my attention is the clause 'his parents could not afford a uniform', in sentence 1. The clause presents a grammatical puzzle: what syntactic analysis do we give to the verb 'afford'? That is, it may be that the grammar of *afford* differs systematically for different groups in a society, so that for certain readers of this paper a transactive reading (that is, where the verb is transitive both syntactically and in meaning) has become naturalized. For these readers (the ability) to afford something is not a state but is an action, a process under the control of an agent, something over which you have control, and which you can cause to happen. For them, to the extent that affording or not affording something is a willed action, under the control of an agent, poverty is self-caused. The other group of readers, for whom the paper has to make provision also, read afford as being non-transactive (that is, syntactically transitive as here, but not transitive in meaning) hence beyond the action of individual agents. For them poverty is not necessarily self-caused. (The syntax of *afford* is in fact more complex than this account indicates: it nearly always occurs with some modal element – *manage* to afford; *able* to afford; *can* afford – and seems more frequent in a negated form; both indicators of a complex socio-grammatical function.)

There are other clauses which, while they seem syntactically transitive, align with the non-transitive, non-transactive reading: 'too poor to pay . . .', (3) 'friends found . . . jumble', (7) 'children should not suffer . . .'; and by a further extension, all those clauses which are clearly neither transactive nor transitive, for instance (3) 'His misery . . . ended when . . .'; (6) 'he missed out educationally . . .'; (9) 'The incident happened in the East Midlands . . . when the boy's family moved into the area'; and so on. Forms which align (or can be taken to align) with the transitive, transactive reading on the other hand are 'too poor to pay [money] for . . .', (3) 'friends found . . . jumble', (2) '[someone] separated the 13 year-old from his parents', (10) 'their son moved schools', and so on. In this context, the clearly transactive forms involving other agents should be mentioned – for instance: 'School banishes boy', for these forms help in setting up an expectation of transactive readings, that is, they project a social world in which actors do act and produce effects.

To draw this together at this point: I am suggesting that the clausal syntax of this newspaper report is such that two groups of readers are each facilitated in a distinctively different reading, which is motivated by and supports a particular social-political position. For the readers who see poverty as basically the responsibility of the poor the clausal syntax surrounding 'could not afford' provides on the one hand a context of a systematic set of similarly ambivalent clausal forms, so that *afford* does not occur as an isolated instance ('too poor to pay [money]', 'friends found . . . jumble', 'children suffer [pain or hardship]'), and on the other hand provides a context of clearly transactive clauses ('School banishes boy', and so on) which facilitate transactive readings for the ambivalent cases.

For the other group of readers, who see poverty not necessarily as self-caused, the clausal syntax surrounding 'could not afford' provides a context of a systematic set of similar clausal forms ('friends found jumble' is *not* transactive, because finding is not a willed action; and 'too poor to pay [money]' is not clearly transactive, as *money* is implied in *pay*).

The fact that many of the forms which can be read transactively can also have a non-transactive reading serves, or can serve, the writer's interest: a syntactic form which can be read in both ways – a syntactic form which can be read as assigning agency to subjects, or which can be read as simply 'involving' subjects – may be what best reflects the writer's interest: on the one hand, it buttresses a political view that wishes to hold the poor responsible for their own poverty; and on the other hand, it serves the writer's interest not to alienate those readers who may be poor, or who have a divergent account of the causes of poverty from his own.

It is important to see, as I have briefly pointed out, that there are patterns of these ambiguous forms (and of clauses with a relational syntax, which tend towards a stative reading – 'things are as they are' – of the linguistic-social world). The patterns set up and facilitate modes of reading. Most of the clauses in these

net-like patterns involve the social participants who are implied
and implicated, entailed in my 'focal' clause – 'his parents could
not afford a uniform': the boy, the parents, the school, the school
authorities, the local education authorities, social security services
and bureaucrats. All of these have a place or set of places in the
complex ideological, educational and social politics of the British
Conservative Government. This has, broadly, entailed – apart
from far more widely ramified politics – a move to destroy the
role and function of local education authorities and of other
institutional social and political structures which are seen as
obstacles to the imposition of centralizing control in order to gain,
in this instance, centralized state control of schools. Part of the
strategy of both the government and of the right-wing press has
been an attempt to undermine the credibility not only of local
governmental structures, but also of all forms of social organization which may provide resistance to the 'modernizing' drive of
the conservative state. Hence for instance, the attack on
'bureaucracy', which is itself seen as a leftover from a 'socialist'
and anachronistic version of a socially responsible state (the
'Nanny State'), and an obstacle to conservative moves aimed at
the 'renovation' of society and of the state.

At this stage I want to suggest that just as the grammar of the
single word *poverty* contained social accounts and explanations of
its own domain, so this report is more, or other than, merely a
report. The report serves the task of explaining the existence of
poverty generally through one instance of poverty. The systematic
use of linguistic forms provides one of the means of articulating
that explanation. Clearly, in the case of a text the explanation is
more complex than in the case of a word. And as I demonstrated
with the ambivalence of *afford*, the divergent ideological positions
of different segments of the paper's audience need to be
accommodated in this.

A complex strategy is at work here: several kinds of groups
have to be accommodated in this explanation of poverty. First
there are those for whom *afford* is a transactive verb. For them
poverty is self-caused, wilful, and that is sufficient explanation.
The systematic uses of transactive verb-forms throughout the
report which clearly assign agency and causal power to the actors
of particular processes, not necessarily related directly or indirectly
to an explanation of poverty, provide a matrix of reading and

explanation which leaves no particular problem. Then there is a second group, who read *afford* transactively, but may be somewhat uneasy about ultimate causes and explanations of poverty. For them the strategy aimed at the third group serves well enough. This is a group which reads *afford* as a non-transactive verb, and poverty not necessarily as self-caused – that is, for this group one may find oneself in poverty, through causes which may be self-caused or not.

This third group is provided with a more complex account of multiple agencies and causation. Through the uses of the syntax of verb forms pointed out so far, the writer of the report distributes social roles and assigns series of agentive syntactic roles. For readers who read *afford* non-transactively this identifies a set of associated culprits, people and institutions to whom ultimate responsibility for the cause of hardship through poverty can be sheeted home. Readers are provided with answers to questions such as 'who are the agents who cause this hardship?', 'who is responsible for this poverty?' The answer is one designed for this group specifically: a group broadly in sympathy with the views and policies of the Conservative Government.

Linguistically, semiotically, this leads to the presence of the clearly, unambiguously transactive clauses in which these agents are identified directly, or implied, in agentless passives: '*School* banishes boy' (headline), (1) 'A school boy was taught . . . [by *teachers*]', (2) 'The 13 year-old was separated . . . [by *teachers*]' (both having the impersonal, 'faceless' agent of the passive deleted), (8) 'It was a very hard-hearted thing to do' (where the embedded clause has a deleted agent, '*Someone* did a hard-hearted thing'), (9) '*local bureaucrats* are not helping them' (where the real culprits are identified), and so on.

In this analysis the agents of the transactive clauses are the members of the demonology of the conservative right: local education authorities, local councils, schools, teachers, bureaucrats. It is they who act oppressively towards the hapless, helpless, powerless individual, both parents and child.

There is a fourth group whose political views are provided for in the report. These are readers who have a non-transactive reading of *afford*, and for whom the a-causal verb syntax of the report (either forms such as 'friends found . . . jumble', 'his misery only ended', 'he missed out educationally'), and relational clauses (such as 'It was distressing for a boy', 'his parents were on income support', and so on) express a pained exasperation. The reading suggested by this syntax for them is something like 'Things are awful, and awful things do happen.'

Readers with directly oppositional views, resistant to the explanatory accounts put forward here, are not accommodated. For instance, my own explanatory account would involve a non-transactive reading of *afford*, and a largely transactive verbal syntax with a different set of agents to that offered in my 'reading three' – identifying government policy, right-wing politics, and particular individuals as agents in the transactive clauses.

However, what is important to recognize is that although this newspaper strongly supports the policies of (the right-wing of) the Conservative Government, and one might therefore suppose that its readers do so too, its explanatory account of poverty is far from simple and homogeneous. As an indication merely, rather than a detailed description, here is a summary of the four 'grammars of poverty' as they are put forward in this newspaper report.

1. Poverty is self-caused; the poor are responsible for their own poverty (*afford* is read as a transactive verb, in a systematic grammatical context where other transactive clauses encourage such a reading).
2. Poverty is the responsibility of the poor; there may be circumstances which have made the situation worse for them (*afford* is read transactively; other causes and agents may be (causally) implicated).
3. Poverty is a situation in which you find yourself; other causes and agents are or may be responsible for your poverty (*afford* is read as non-transactive; other causes and agents are causally implicated).
4. Poverty is a situation in which you find yourself; it can happen to anyone (*afford* is read as non-transactive; other processes in the world are also like that).

Transactive	*Non-transactive*
School banishes boy	A boy cannot pay
1 Teachers teach a boy on his own	
2 Teachers separate a 13 year-old	2 His parents could not afford
8 Teachers did a hard-hearted thing	uniform
10 Education chiefs told them	3 His misery ended

Transactive
11 The association revealed the case
12 Local bureaucrats are not helping
   poor children
   etc.

Non-transactive
3   Friends found jumble
6   He missed out
7   Children should not suffer
    like this
    They cannot afford a uniform
    The incident happened
    The boy's family moved
10 They did not qualify
12 Poor children are suffering
    etc.

Relational
   A boy is too poor
4   'It is the worst case'
5   'It was distressing'
10 His parents were on income
    support

A fourth category consists of those clauses which can be read differently by different groups.

2   His parents could not afford uniform
3   Friends found jumble
7   Children should not suffer (pain, anguish) like this

A brief scan reveals the class of agents in the transactive category, acting to cause hardship and poverty: *schools, teachers, education chiefs, local bureaucrats, local authorities*. The class of participants who are simply involved, the passive sufferers of the actions caused by these agents are *boy, parents, friends, children, poor children*, and so on. The category of relational clauses supports this last category, people are in certain states of affairs: 'a boy is too poor', 'his parents were on income support', and so on.

The reading which makes *afford* into a transactive has the effect of leaving the first category as it is other than to add *parents* into it, so that they become a part of the group acting wilfully to bring about misery. The syntax thus clearly represents some facets of conservative discourse. There are, of course, other readings at other times, and these are by no means complementary or compatible. So the transactive reading of 'his parents could not afford' is a politically conservative reading, which assigns responsibility for 'their' poverty to the poor. In other texts, not represented here, but which occur on other occasions in this newspaper, schools and teachers are represented as sites and agents of heroic resistance to (socialist) local council tyranny, through the agency of parent power. Of course, these kinds of contradictions within common sense are exactly what we should expect.

My description provides an explanation of this seemingly confused and contradictory syntactic pattern at the level of the clause, and of the overall text, in terms of the interests of the producer of the text, namely the wish to provide a particular set of accounts of poverty, both as *caused* (by heartless bureaucrats and so on), and as *uncaused* (something which simply is, in which people *are*). And it allows those readers who wish to do so, to assign responsibility to the poor, to the parents who could but do not wish to afford the uniform. The writer's interest in structuring the text in terms of the perceptions of the text by its envisaged readers is of course one significant interest. The complexities of that possible reception, which includes divergent audiences with divergent interests, are coded in the complex sign of the text, and in the smaller-level signs of clause and sentence.

The micro-history of the production and readings of this text is set in the context of the macro-history of British society and of the British state at this time. The text also embodies that social state, and in doing so deproblematizes and naturalizes that state of affairs by providing a set of explanations, which derive their efficacy from operating relatively covertly, and nearly invisibly.

More could be said about this text. What I wish to do now, before turning to a discussion of the other reports on this page is to turn attention briefly to the question of boundaries. Is the text which I have just discussed complete of itself, bounded and discrete, or is it to be read and understood as a part of a larger unit? It is only one of (at least) five discrete texts on this page, and the question arises whether the other units jointly taken as a larger text, as *the* text, provide yet a further explanation of poverty. Do we need to think of the text in a much enlarged fashion in order to arrive at a full reading of a text?

My answer is 'Probably yes and no'. The question of the boundaries of texts and of the boundaries of reading have hardly begun to be addressed; but they are some of the most urgent questions in the study of texts and of reading. The report which I have just analysed was written, in all likelihood, as a free-standing piece; with the knowledge nevertheless that it would appear on a page together with other pieces, and probably in the knowledge that the person responsible for the layout of the page would attempt to construct a page that made a certain sense.

Nor can we know, other than through the observation of a particular reader, how the piece is read, as I mentioned in my discussion of the reading path followed by a given reader. In a theory of reading we need to make provision for both possibilities; namely that any one reader may simply read this one text and take no notice of any other aspect of the page, or that she or he may read more than one piece and may attempt to make sense of them together. In the second case the issue is still not settled, because many readers have absorbed rules about boundaries, namely that a text is bounded by conventionally agreed boundary signs, and is not to be read in conjunction with other texts. We need to know something about the reading conventions which individual readers (have been taught to) adopt, as well as about the structure of texts.

An adequate theory of reading will be able to accommodate itself to the reader's decision about what constitutes a text, and at the same time be able to recognize the structurings of text, at all levels, which producers of texts use to organize and structure the readings of readers.

Given that assumption I could leave the analysis of the report as an analysis of a complete text, always providing that one particular reader had dealt with this text in this fashion. However, my assumption also takes account of the possibility of a reader's going beyond the single text, and of the decisions of the person who did the layout of the page to construct the *page* as a meaningful unit. In the next two sections I will concern myself with readings which treat the page as a unit of meaning, both for the producer and, potentially, for the reader.

The visual representation of poverty and hardship

The 'School banishes boy' report is framed by two other stories of hardship. One, an upbeat one, reports the reward of Supermum Freda, who has, for nine years, fostered 'child victims of abuse'. The other, not upbeat, reports a plea to the Chancellor on behalf of a car manufacturer and all those suffering from 'increased costs for company car users'. The first, the photonews report, consists of three images – one large image of the Duchess of Kent with 'Lucky Lucinda', one large image of the Duchess with Lucky Lucinda and Esther Rantzen, a media personality, and one small image of Freda Mawhinney. It is a report, visually and verbally, about caring: of institutions and individuals caring for other individuals; individuals who happen to be members of the royal family, a clergyman, the media, 'Supermum Freda', and 'Lucky Lucinda' – not an abused child as it turns out, but the daughter of a former employee of the media personality; BT (the privatized British Telecom) which provides the £7700 in awards; and 'Streetwise Youth', a voluntary organization.

The hardship reported here is kept rigorously at a distance: what is foregrounded are the rewards of caring (though it is not quite clear why 'Lucky Lucinda' is being rewarded): cuddles, acclaim and money. The report takes up about two-fifths of the page in size, larger than the 'School banishes boy' report. What is backgrounded, indeed what is absent, is the subject of hardship. In the visual text, there is no mention, no sign or trace of those who are the victims of hardship (Lucinda not being an abused child); though there is visual evidence of 'caring' – the child sitting on the Duchess's knee. Even in the brief verbal text with the larger photonews report there is just one mention of 'child victims of abuse'. There is thus a complete contrast between this report, and the 'School banishes boy' report. In the latter, those suffering hardship are very much present; and agency is a strongly present issue, even if overall it is made highly complex and fuzzy. In the photonews report those suffering hardship are absent, and with their absence goes an absence of concern with agency in relation to hardship.

The visual story is about something altogether different: it is about elements of the state, institutions, individuals or representatives of institutions shown, publicly, to care; or at least, to care publicly. Hence the much larger space given over to the photos of the Duchess and Esther Rantzen, compared with that of the only real agent in this report, Freda Mawhinney. In its internal structuring there is a contrast between the bottom picture and the top picture, both formally/grammatically and in terms of their content. The bottom photograph has a clear setting: it is in a room, with recognizable furniture, and above all with some action

– even if this is a staged action. People are doing things: talking, reading, looking, yawning. In the top image there is no context, the details of the setting are lost in the medium close-up shot. And nor are people doing things: the Duchess's gaze goes to some object to the right.

In the bottom image we are in the world of the real, of actions, of processes and events. In the top photo we are no longer in the same world of the real. The gaze of the Duchess is out of time: she just is, and cares. Where the bottom image has specificity, the top image has generality, or even an idealized aspect: the royal family, as *the* family in the state, caring. In the verbal text between these two images, actions are, as in one reading of the 'School banishes boy' report, not clearly transactive: 'receiving acclaim', 'expecting acclaim', 'sharing an award', 'enjoying a cuddle'. The real core of action and cause for this event, Freda Mawhinney's care of the children, is completely displaced and negated, in the photonews report overall as much as in details of the verbal/clausal syntax. So for instance, Freda's actions in her care for children are doubly displaced: from her to her house 'Freda's home . . . has been open house' (rather than 'Freda opened her home'), and from an action – opening the house, or caring for children – to a state – her home has *been* open house, her house *is* open; and thus effectively negating this woman's work over the years.

In this report, attention is firmly moved away from the private person Freda to the public figures of the Duchess of Kent and the media personality Esther Rantzen. This is expressed as much through the relative size of the images, as it is through more lexical/iconographic aspects, such as positioning of the respective 'participants' in the image – the Duchess, Esther Rantzen, Freda Mawhinney – the directionality of their gaze. For instance, to take the feature 'proximity', whereas Freda Mawhinney's photograph is at close-up, both Esther Rantzen and the Duchess at their closest are in a medium-long shot to long-shot. This brings Freda into the domain of close proximity to readers, a distance suggestive of interactions of the private domain; whereas both Esther Rantzen and the Duchess remain at a much more formal, public distance.

If we consider the photonews report to consist of three elements, which I'll call 'Lucky Lucinda' (LL), 'Supermum' (Freda), and 'So rewarding' (SR), respectively, the Duchess is placed at the left of each of the two images in which she appears; Freda's image is at the right of the element in which it appears. An aspect of the significance of this left-right structuring can be appreciated by a comparison with the 'Car boss' report. It has a similar structure, of (near) close-up image plus text. Here, however, the image is on the left, giving it a different semiotic (grammatical) function and status: something akin to 'source of the story', 'author of the comment'. Freda, by contrast, is presented as an 'instance' of the private citizen who receives official 'acclaim'. Left-most position carries a different set of meanings to right-most position; in *Reading Images* (Kress and van Leeuwen 1990) their difference is characterized as, very broadly speaking, a distinction of 'given' and 'new' – where 'given' can have more specific meanings: 'established', 'uncontentious', 'known', 'taken for granted', 'understood by viewers', and so on. These in turn can be given even greater specificity, as in the 'Car boss' report, where this range of meanings is made more specific, as 'author', 'authored by', and hence 'authoritative'.

The contrast with Freda's position in that textual element becomes clearer from this; as does the positioning of the Duchess in the photograph, in left-most position. There she represents the 'taken for granted', 'authoritative', 'known', 'generally understood', so that the other values and meanings attributed to her in the report are embedded in this set of meanings.

The visual structure of the photonews overall and of the components of this report thus conveys a whole set of meanings, quite other than those conveyed in the captions and in the brief verbal report. The images are not simply 'illustrations' of what is said in other ways in the verbal report. The images convey quite other meanings: about participation; about the participants' social position (private and public); their power (expressed, for instance, in the angle at which the photos are taken: front on or from low to high for participants in LL and SR, and down, high to low for Freda); about their centrality or marginality in public life; and so on.

To this we must add the effect of the top-bottom structuring of this report. In general this can be characterized as a disappearance of the objects of hardship, a denial or negation by non-mention; and a focus on a more abstracted, 'higher', level at which these issues are dealt with at a great remove. 'Higher' is signalled both by the move from private to public, from individual to institution, and by invoking the 'highest' institution in the nation, the monarchy. It is also signalled by the layout structure of the photonews report, with the more general, abstracted, image in the structural position of 'the ideal' in visual images.

The grammar of the page: poverty in the widest context

More can be said about these two reports; and more could be said particularly about the texts I have not discussed. However I will now move to a very brief discussion of the grammar of the whole page. That is, if we take my earlier hypothesis seriously, namely that the strategy of layout is to construct the page as the relevant unit of meaning, and that this strategy may also be that of many readers – even if differences in reading strategies occur within that – then we need to have some formal means of describing how either the producer of the page or a particular reader make their sense of the page.

The left-right, top-bottom structure which I mentioned earlier applies to the page as a whole. The large headline across the top of the right half of the page gives prominence to the 'top', and marks the distinction of top versus bottom. There is a rough division of the page, marked by a band formed by the 'Supermum' element and by the top of the advertisement, which also produces a division of top section of the page versus bottom section of the page. Similarly, with the left-right opposition, which is even more clearly marked than the top-bottom opposition. The question is, in terms of the page as a unit, which is being marked by this structure?

To take the top-bottom distinction first. The two main elements in the top section are the image of the Duchess with Lucky Lucinda, and the bold headline. Each provides a compressed explanation. The image, as I mentioned, is an abstracted, generalized account of 'care'; and as the figure of the Duchess will be well known to readers, its meaning is read together with 'feminine care', to produce the meaning – however briefly, swiftly, imprecisely apprehended – of 'the caring royals', 'the royal family cares'. The headline produces a meaning, again no matter how imprecisely apprehended and articulated, of oppression of individuals by heartless institutions. This meaning will be familiar to readers of this newspaper; and the specific institution involved, a school, will be familiar as a target for reproach from, at this time, general and widespread attacks on all institutional aspects of the education system.

The sharp contrast between these two readings itself forms a message: the caring state (through its apolitical representative in this case) and the problematic, unregenerate, heartless, institutions which prove to be obstacles to the general and widespread effects of the benevolent influence of the state.

So far the reader who reads no more than this top section, whose reading path usually takes her or him to the top of the page – the structural place of the message of the page in its ideal form – that is the meaning that she or he will get from the page. For that reader the bottom half will be the relatively more specific, detailed, messy account of the actual real-world correspondences to that ideal world. Of course he or she may catch sight of the 'Car boss' report, and become aware of the hardship suffered by other sections of society. That may be one reason for placing that story there.

The left-right structure of the page takes the reader from the given, understood, uncontentious visual statement 'There is care' – provided by individuals and institutions, from a member of the royal family, British Telecom, and a 'Supermum' – to the report which indicates that this taken-for-granted situation still harbours areas of problems, in the heartless actions of bureaucratic institutions and individuals who are relics from the oppressive socialist state machinery. Tucked into that story, in layout, is the story about the hardship suffered by car industry bosses and by those who cannot so readily get a company car.

The top-bottom structure of the page tells a different aspect of this story: the top segment has aspects of the meanings of the left-right structure in a general and/or idealized, abstracted form. I have already mentioned the meaning of the top element of the photonews report. The top-most element of the central report is the large headline: it condenses the complex elements of the report below into two elements: an individual suffers or is made to suffer twice – through the uncaring action of a school, and through his poverty, in that order. This unites the explanation of poverty with an attack on the education establishment. The bottom part of the page provides the detail on which these abstractions are based, in each case.

In this broad sketch I am aware that I have made no mention of the advertisement for the film. Reading it simply as a part of this page – I do not know the film – it fits well enough into this scheme. If the right is the side of instances of the still problematic present in the context of an underlying benevolent situation, and if the bottom is the segment of the (messy) detail, then, simply on the basis of the visual and textual aspects of this advertisement/text, it does not disrupt the reading of the page I have put forward so far.

The last point I wish to make in relation to a reading of the page has to do with the modal aspects of the different structural components of this page. In a straightforward contrast of visual and verbal components of the page as a message, photographs have a higher modality/factuality status than language. Photographs, in this kind of commonsense reading, carry their own guarantee of authenticity and veracity: they seem literally just to report what is there in the world. The photonews report thus carries not only the meanings conveyed by the leftmost place in the left-right, given–new structure of the page, it also appears in the semiotic mode which has highest modal value, and this carries the greatest degree of factualness. That is, among other things, also one effect of the entirely ubiquitous use of the small close-ups of individuals, as in the case of Supermum Freda, and car boss Paul Tosch.

Into this broad meaning-structure are read the detailed explanations of hardship and poverty. This leads to layerings of reading, which proceed from large chunkings to detail, in an order which depends on an individual's habituated reading path, and which establishes most crucially what elements are read first and therefore have that priority, and what elements are read later, and therefore can more likely form elaborations of the initial element. From these large chunkings and their quickly provided reading frames, a reader may then move to the complexities of the detail, which are by then already inevitably being read in terms of the reading frame initially provided. From there a reader is likely to go back to big chunkings again, which at that point once more provide larger frames of ordering.

This is in no way to suggest that reading is anarchic: even though a reader may not follow the writer's or the page-layout person's intended structurings, these structurings (at all levels) provide the frames within which readings are constructed. The details of individual readings will be guided by the structurings of the page; so that while there are likely to be individual differences in actual readings, these are in a range which is predictable from the structurings of the elements of the page, and of the page as a whole.

What then, is the explanation of hardship and of poverty which this page offers? Without any real question the two major texts are the photonews report and the 'School banishes boy' report. The other textual elements ('Earlobe risk', the advertisement, and 'Car boss's plea') have an important rhetorical function in that they fill in an overall picture which says that everyone suffers hardship, of all kinds, everywhere. That is a significant element of the account of hardship. The central account, however, is made up of the two major reports. And these define, pretty well, the range of accounts within a Conservative Party view.

Depending on the reader's reading path, these broadly consist (with initial focus on the 'School banishes boy' report) of the range of accounts I described above, from 'the poor are responsible for their poverty' to 'there are instances of poverty, caused in the end by uncaring, heartless institutions and individuals'. All these together define the problem that is at the centre, to be dealt with. The context is provided by the photonews report, which shows individuals of high rank – and also of low, in the case of Freda Mawhinney – and institutions 'caring': there *is* care. With a reading path which focuses initially on the photonews report, this provides the core of the account, 'things are as they are, by and large: there is care', but it then goes on to outline the problems that remain and identifies the causes of the problem.

The photonews report, in the position of 'given', in the end probably provides the decisive anchoring of the possible readings for members of the *Daily Express*'s audience. It provides readers with the information that 'yes, there is hardship everywhere, all of us are affected, no one is getting away without some suffering, and there are still some political battles to be fought'. But in all this, the ground of the explanatory account, the left of the page, the report with the highest factuality reading, gives readers the reassuring information that at bottom things are well in hand, in a fundamentally caring society.

References and further reading

Fairclough, N. (1988) *Language and Power*. London: Longman.

Fowler, R. G. (1992) *News Discourse*. London: Routledge.

Hodge, R. I. V. and Kress, G. R. (1988) *Social Semiotics*. Cambridge: Polity Press.

Hodge, R. I. V. and Kress, G. R. (1992) *Language as Ideology* (revised edition). London: Routledge.

Kress, G. R. (1989) *Linguistic Processes in Sociocultural Practice*. Oxford: Oxford University Press.

Kress, G. R. and van Leeuwen, T. (1990) *Reading Images*. Geelong, Victoria: Deakin University Press.

Kress, G. R. and van Leeuwen, T. (1994) *Reading Images: The Design of Visual Communication*. London: Routledge.

Lee, D. A. (1992) *Competing Discourses*. London: Longman.

2 The international dimension

Brian Street

Introduction

I want to consider the relationship between representations of 'poverty' in the United Kingdom context and recent accounts, in the British media, of poverty in the Third World. It is arguable that until recently the representation of British poverty was rooted in images of this country's recent past, notably the Depression – cobbled streets, urchins without shoes, the black and white photographs of *Picture Post* and the Mass-Observation project on Bolton. Other chapters in this book highlight some of this imagery and examine how it is incorporated and modified in contemporary discourses. It could be argued that much of the critique of the *Breadline Britain* programme and the NALGO advertisements cited in the Introduction and below was premised on notions of how 'true' poverty should be represented and that these earlier images represented the touchstone against which that truth was to be judged.

Today, however, there is a competing set of images and discourses on poverty – those associated with the Third World. I would like to suggest that the narratives of poverty in Britain during this period might have been constructed – implicitly and explicitly – with reference to this international dimension. The notion of 'constructed' is crucial here: as Kress has argued in the previous chapter, the new ways of 'reading' texts with which this volume is concerned require us to understand them in relation to their 'context'. In attempting to answer the question both of what a text brings to the reader and what a reader brings to a text, we need to analyse the concepts constructed by both text and reader prior to their immediate interaction. I am suggesting that in the context of texts about poverty in the UK, a notion of 'Third World poverty' is being constructed by other texts and that this construct then provides part of what a reader brings to the UK texts and of what is available – often implicitly – to be read in those texts.

Much of the evidence for this is circumstantial – the texts on Third World poverty appear in the same media during the same period as those on poverty in the UK. But there are also some specific cross-references, as I shall detail below, where the account of poverty in the UK is explicitly linked by the producers of the text with that in the Third World. My data, then, are textual in the specific sense that they comprise media reports during a particular period. My argument is suggestive: to take it further and to assert it more conclusively, would require further and different evidence, both greater coverage of media reporting over a longer period and material such as the accounts of reader and viewer response provided by Richardson (Chapter 4) or of participants' own views on poverty, hinted at by Hewitt (Chapter 5).

The methodological justification for this approach is in part derived from the principles of case study research described by Mitchell (1984) for social anthropology. He distinguishes between two kinds of analytical inference from case studies: 'The first is that of inferring that relationships observed in a sample of instances available to the analyst exist in the wider population from which the sample has been drawn' (p. 239) – the 'typicality' or 'representativeness' to which the programme makers of *Breadline Britain* occasionally appeal and on which much sociological research is grounded. The second kind of inference is somewhat different and it is this kind to which the present chapter (and much of the present book) appeals: 'This is the inference that the *theoretical* relationship among conceptually defined elements in the sample will also apply in the parent population. The basis of an inference of this sort is the cogency of the theoretical argument linking the elements in an intelligible way rather than the statistical representativeness of the sample' (p. 239). This argument is important in the present instance both for an understanding of what this chapter and much of the volume are trying to accomplish but also because it provides a way of reading the aims of the producers of *Breadline Britain*, which forms such an important part of our database. As Mitchell argues, 'From this point of view, the search for a "typical" case for analytical exposition is likely to be less fruitful than the search for a "telling" case in which the particular circumstances surrounding a case serve to make previously obscure theoretical relationships apparent' (p. 139).

The theoretical question with which I am concerned is 'what is poverty?' That is a question debated among the subjects with whom we are concerned, whether programme makers, television viewers or newspaper reporters. As the authors of this volume, we are also concerned with other questions: how are texts read and in the present case, how are texts on poverty read? What does the reader bring to them and what does the text bring to the reader? The kinds of data I bring to bear on these questions – mainly newspaper reports in the selected period, but also some reference to television news reports and to historical constructions of poverty in the UK – can, I hope, help to answer these questions in the way that Mitchell suggests:

> Case Studies used in this way are clearly more than 'apt illustrations'. Instead they are the means whereby general theory may be developed ... What the anthropologist using a case study to support an argument does is to show how general principles deriving from some theoretical orientation manifest themselves in some given set of particular circumstances. A good case study, therefore, enables the analyst to establish theoretically valid connections between events and phenomena which were previously ineluctable. (p. 139)

The connections I am looking for in this case are those between international perspectives on poverty provided in various media accounts on the one hand and, on the other, representations of poverty within the UK, both in the media and in the sociological literature that underpins some at least of the media reporting. That the connections are theoretically valid is, I argue, suggested – if not yet firmly established – by an account grounded in the theories of text and context set out in this volume. Such a finding generates the possibility of further research into the reading of poverty along these lines – thus helping us to understand representations of this specific phenomenon more richly, and also demonstrating ways in which new theories of text may be theoretically developed and empirically applied, whether to poverty or to other phenomena.

As other papers in this volume demonstrate, the representations of poverty in the British media during the period under consideration tended to focus on two debates: the definition of poverty itself, whether it should be conceived as absolute or as relative; and the truth or falsity of the attempts to represent and illustrate 'poverty' through real life examples. Both debates are dependent, of course, on the position of the particular parties that construct them and there is no 'neutral' account. I am interested, though, in the availability of particular discourses for representing those interests. I argue that while these discourses are, of course, themselves constructed by interest groups, there is also a longer-term and less evidently manipulable basis for them than is attested by a focus merely on the immediate interest of particular groups. The persistence over time of specific discourses – historical discourses on poverty in the UK and international discourses on poverty in the Third World – makes it harder to challenge specific debates – such as the absolute/relative one or the truth/falsity one: it is harder to shift a discourse than it is to construct an agenda for debate within one. New discourses do, however, emerge – not so much through conscious machinations in the way that such agendas might be constructed as through the combination of social and ideological and discursive forces (Fairclough 1985). I want to argue here that a new discourse is becoming available for representing poverty that may have profound effects on the agendas themselves. That discourse involves the use of international comparison to locate specific issues in one's own country, and includes the presentation of supposedly comparable empirical data from other countries in order to highlight features of the home society. This is a new 'discourse' in the sense that it combines sets of signs, mainly linguistic but also visual and semiotic, in a relatively coherent and socially significant way.

In this case, the representation of 'poverty' in Third World countries, accompanied by specific images in print and visual media, serves to complicate the debates in the UK over relative and absolute poverty and over the truth and falsity of representation. In a sense, this new discourse shifts both debates towards a supposedly more universalistic account against which the arguments of both sides in the UK context can be represented by their opponents as relatively trivial. Although the immediate concern is to win points within a given debate, in practice the new discourse begins to undermine the basis on which the argument is being made. I will attempt to justify this claim through reference to newspaper articles and pictures during the period under consideration (and shortly afterwards). It will also be important to place this material in broader historical context: accounts of working-class life in Britain have long drawn on images of life in other societies, particularly in the recent Imperial past (Mackenzie 1986), and the discourse I am attempting to describe is not radically new, although I would want to argue that it takes on specific form in the present time. Again the 'context' for the texts which we are considering involves the construct not only of 'Third World Poverty' – the international dimension that is the main thrust of this paper – but also of 'Poverty in the recent British past' – the historical dimension that many of the respondents in Richardson's and Hewitt's accounts refer to. An analysis of the semantic field encompassed by the term 'poverty' requires, I argue, some attention to both of these dimensions.

Definitions of 'poverty' in sociology and the media

The definition of 'poverty' in the UK, at least since the post-war era, has hinged on debates about whether it is absolute or relative. In the post-war era it was briefly assumed that poverty had been overcome as living standards rose and as it appeared that the working class were becoming middle class (Westergaard 1972). The embourgeoisment thesis dominated sociological literature and the popular imagination for some time, fed by empirical accounts such as that of the Luton car workers (Lockwood et al. 1958) who appeared to be adopting middle-class tastes, buying formerly 'luxury' goods such as washing machines and refrigerators and even shifting their voting behaviour in line with images of class mobility (cf. Goldthorpe 1969). The absolute poverty of the pre-war era was seen to be gone for ever and Britain was now an 'affluent' society. The welfare state was needed only to provide a safety net for the few who could not manage. This view was strongly challenged from the outset by a number of radical sociologists (Coates and Silburn 1970; Westergaard 1972) who provided both theoretical and empirical studies to show that poverty was still endemic in British society, both in its extreme pre-war sense and also in a new way, through a sense of 'relative deprivation'. Townsend (1979) and others argued that the sense of worth and position through which people's social identity was constructed involved comparison with others, so that at a period when many were certainly more affluent, those who were falling behind had a more acute sense of their hardship by contrast. Townsend drew up a series of indices of relative poverty, ranging from availability of toilets and bathrooms in people's homes, to the opportunity for family holidays and for other ways of partaking in the new 'affluent' society. Media images and advertisements for consumer goods, figuring what it meant to be a member of post-war British society, reinforced for many their sense that they were not part of this development. That, according to commentators such as Townsend and Coates, was what effectively constituted 'poverty' at that time.

The Nuffield studies of social mobility (Goldthorpe et al. 1980) similarly showed that although there had been some shift in absolute mobility – that is, more people were moving up the class hierarchy according to various measures, such as occupation, compared with their parents – there was still a greater chance of achieving a good job, desired housing, disposable income if one's parents already had these things – that is relative mobility had not changed so much as absolute mobility. There was nothing like perfect mobility in which life chances were the same for each new child – chances still varied according to background, parental income and position in the class structure. The British class structure itself had not altered, only the movement of some groups within it had become a little more fluid. In a famous image Goldthorpe (1980) suggested this was like the movement in and out of the carriages of a train: there may be more movement between carriages, but the carriages themselves remain different from each other.

The media representations under consideration in the present study draw upon this academic literature, both explicitly and implicitly. The popular press favoured concrete focus on the indices of poverty, particularly housing conditions, clothing and food, with particular attention to children. The *Daily Mirror* (8.4.91) ran a headline 'Eleven Million on the breadline in Britain' with sub-heads: 'Kids Go Hungry' and 'No home heating'. The associated articles used statistics drawn from the *Breadline Britain* survey: 'About 2½ million youngsters go without proper food and are dressed in second-hand clothes; ten million people live in houses that are damp or without heating; seven million lack essential clothing like a warm water proof coat.' While these items drew on popular images of absolute poverty, partly through the use of terms such as 'proper' and 'essential', the article also makes use of the Townsend index of relative poverty, citing for instance that 'About 6½ million cannot afford household goods such as carpets, a fridge or a phone', items that would not have figured in a pre-war index. They also refer to relative indices through comparison of income figures over the previous eight years – 'The poor's income in the Tory years has fallen by nearly 5 per cent while the rich have seen theirs rocket by 40 per cent.'

The Guardian, addressing a more middle-class and academic readership than the *Daily Mirror*, is more self-conscious about the existence of different ways of measuring poverty, but draws on the same discourses. A leader on 8.4.91 cites a European Commission report which suggests that, '*On the report's definitions*, some 10.3 million people, or 3.8 million households, were living in poverty in Britain in the middle eighties.' In an article in the same paper, the Social Services Correspondent notes that, '*The poverty yardstick used by the researchers* was households with disposable income less than 50 per cent of the national average' (my emphasis). This is a relative measure in two senses; first, that the poverty threshold is a statistical one, meaning that there will always be some people by definition living in poverty; secondly, the survey compares poverty on this index with previous surveys and also as between different countries.

> According to the Teekens figures [in an EC survey], 49 million EC residents were living in poverty in 1980 and 50 million in 1985. Of these 8.2 million in 1980 and 10.3 million (18.2 per cent) in 1985 were in the UK, representing 2.8 million and 3.8 million households respectively.
>
> By household, the UK moves from the 8th poorest to the 2nd poorest EC state . . . By 1985 the UK accounted for 23.5 per cent of all EC households living below their respective national poverty lines.

The article, however, also notes the dispute over measures of poverty: 'The Government has consistently opposed the commission's use of a poverty benchmark and has won adoption of a broader definition of poverty for the current, third European poverty programme ... The Department of Social Security said: "This whole concept of a poverty line is regarded by ministers as rather absurd, taking no account of differences between countries in demography or labour market trends"' (a position that opens the way to favourable comparison of the UK with Third World countries).

The newspaper also addresses the measures being used for the London Weekend Television (LWT) series *Breadline Britain 1990s*, which arrives at a broadly similar verdict by a different route – people's own perceptions. LWT used 'a MORI survey which first asked respondents what amenities they *considered* the essentials of a decent life and went on to calculate how many people in Britain fall short' (my emphasis). The methodological focus in this survey, then, was on subjective views of what constituted 'poverty', while the European Commission used more objective measures, though still within a broadly relative definition of poverty. The MORI survey produced a figure of '11 million people, including three million children, living in poverty' and again the relative dimension is introduced by comparison with an earlier date – 'a 50 per cent increase in the numbers uncovered in a previous survey in 1983'.

The representation of poverty

The bulk of the coverage in the press during this period, however, did not explicitly address (though many did so implicitly) either the conceptual issue of how to define poverty nor the substantive issue of whether poverty, however defined, was increasing in the UK. Rather, it took issue with the attempts by some groups to illustrate the concrete experience of poverty through various forms of representation. The *Breadline Britain* programme was one such attempt. But during the same period there was also major media coverage of an advertisement campaign by the health union NALGO. NALGO's intention in this campaign was to draw attention to what the union perceived as failings in the government's health policy that were leading to hardship and poverty, through advertisements that represented individuals suffering. One pictured a Down's syndrome sufferer with a caption claiming he was 'one of the 480,000 people made homeless last year'. Another showed an infant with a caption claiming she was born prematurely, weighing 2½ lb: she desperately needs an incubator, we are told, but 'Unfortunately, so does the hospital'. An advertisement depicting a school featured a haunting portrait of a young girl 'spending six hours a day in a freezing room. The walls are crumbling. And sometimes there's no-one to look after her. It can be tough at school.'

The people used for the portraits were paid by professional photographers to represent the theme and were themselves not necessarily in the condition described and it is this that much of the tabloid press coverage chose to focus on. The Down's syndrome sufferer, according to the *Daily Mail*, 'lives comfortably with his mother and brother Sam in their well-furnished, warm house'; the schoolgirl, according to the same newspaper, goes to a 'clean, warm school'; the baby, according to the *Daily Express*, 'had not needed an incubator and weighed almost 5 lb'. The newspapers dwelt on the issue of representation and truth, tracking down photographic agencies, 'shocked' mothers and teachers to deny the 'truth' of the pictures and headlining their articles: 'Lies', 'Propaganda', 'Sham'. Much weight was placed on the fact that those photographed were often paid by a commercial agency: the *Daily Express*, for instance, featured a quote by the mother of the baby: ' "It was explained that Georgia would be in an advert but I didn't know exactly what the advert would be", said Mrs Okoro, 29, of South London, who was paid £300' (2.5.92). Two (possibly contradictory) themes are thereby merged – the notion that the mother was deceived (and, by extension, the public) and the fact that the mother took money (as did other 'victims', such as in the *Breadline Britain* programme) as though this implied collusion with the advertiser's deception.

A leader in the *Evening Standard* (2.5.91) likewise indicates the discursive strategies employed in the media to handle this 'story' – framing under a truth/lies heading: counterpointing description of a picture with 'in fact' statements that supposedly confirm the objective truth; locating the issue in an Advertising Standards context rather than a Health Service one; and invoking the 'voices' of participants as reasonable observers, thereby disguising the voice of the newspaper itself as an opinion expresser and constructor of the story. Under the headline: 'NALGO and its Lies' the leader states:

NALGO's series of advertisements in the national Press, containing blatant inaccuracies designed to attract Labour voters in the local elections, has cost the union's membership some £500,000. One advertisement showed a picture of a baby and claimed that it needed an incubator that was not available because of NHS underfunding. In fact, the baby shown was perfectly healthy and had not needed an incubator at any stage. Another advertisement showed a girl whose school was said to be freezing and crumbling. In fact, the school was well-heated and in good condition and the furious headmistress is considering a complaint to the Advertising Standards Authority.

The *Evening Standard*'s 'news' article on the issue reproduces the advertisement picture of the girl with the caption: 'The caption for this Nalgo advert claims: "This girl spends six hours a day in a freezing room." It was posed by a model.' The reference to the Nalgo 'caption' disguises the fact that the *Evening Standard* has in fact put its own – alternative – caption under the picture; and again the juxtaposition of 'this advert claims' against the truth statement 'It was posed', serves to make it seem as though the newspaper is providing objective facts while the advertisement is engaged in sententious assertion.

Even if a reader disagrees with a newspaper's position on the substantive issues regarding the decline or increase of poverty, they would find it hard against these discursive strategies to avoid being drawn into acceptance of the agenda for debate – that the issue is one of truth versus lies and of the morality of advertising. The substantive issues regarding poverty raised by both the NALGO advertisements and the *Breadline Britain* programme are not addressed. The detailed figures quoted by *The Guardian* and the debate over relative and absolute poverty are subverted by the attention to representation, in this case pictorial images and the truth they supposedly convey. If the 'concrete' images of poverty turn out not to be true, then the poverty they purport to represent may also be untrue. Both are lies and a sham.

The international dimension

These discourses and debates about poverty in the UK provide the background and the context within which I now wish to consider representations of Third World poverty in the media during the same period. During the ten days from Wednesday, 24 April 1991 to Sunday, 5 May, newspapers reported on major catastrophes in four areas of the world: the Kurds' plight in fleeing from Saddam Hussein; a cyclone in Bangladesh and famine in Ethiopia (reported together on the front page of *The Guardian* on 3 May under a headline 'Twin Disasters Hit Third World'); and accounts of an 'imminent catastrophe' in southern Africa following a prolonged drought. Although it might appear that the sheer numbers and magnitude of crises in the Third World during this period were exceptional, the point is that against the tidal wave of this reporting, the occasional shots of the homeless in London and the debates over 'fabricated' accounts of poverty in Britain as a whole could appear relatively minor. The images remain even after the immediate story has passed off the front page. Many of the reports either replicated general imagery and terminology familiar for Third World 'poverty' irrespective of place and time, or were repeated at a later date in magazine as opposed to news coverage, recycling and thereby reinforcing many of the images and terms that had first appeared on the front pages.

The Bangladesh cyclone was reported to have killed possibly 100,000 people and *The Guardian* reported on the front page, alongside a photograph of ragged youths standing astride the rubble of their houses, that the country had 'launched a desperate appeal for international assistance'. The effects were 'devastating', the 'scale of the destruction far greater than any previous national disasters' and the aftermath would require 'the international community to launch a massive relief operation as they did for the Kurdish refugees'. The comparisons here are with other 'disasters' both in that country and, recognizably to readers that day, following the Gulf War. The language appears appropriately heightened in response to the numbers involved and the scale of the destruction; and the issue is one for the international community. This style of representation makes the reporting on poverty in Britain appear, in contrast, technical and academic – comparing numbers with previous eras of British history or debating systems of measurement, as we have seen. Nor is the other 'home' debate – truth/lies – addressed in the international context, again implying that the meaning and seriousness of the term 'poverty' in that domain is self-evident. The text and the context bring to the reader the framing message that the agendas within which poverty in the UK is debated are relatively insignificant beside these major international 'catastrophes'.

That the international discourse is about 'poverty' and not just natural disasters which might not bear comparison with the UK, is brought home in a number of reports. In a *Guardian* report on the International News page (3.5.91), for instance, Michael Simmons writes 'Poverty, not tidal wave, is real killer in Bangladesh'. The point being made here was that the climate only has these devastating effects because of the cruel poverty in which the population is living: the poor have nowhere else to go and are living on low lying land that is constantly subject to flooding on this scale: 'According to United Nations estimates, nearly 20 million people – one in six of the population – living on about 15 per cent of the land area are threatened with "total inundation" if the sea level rises by 5 feet. Another 10 million would be affected if the rise were about 10 feet.' This is 'poverty', articulated through pictures, statistics and academic analyses and the headline declares it as such. The concepts of disaster, catastrophe, famine are seen not as independent phenomena to arouse horror and sympathy but as linked with 'poverty' thus giving the term a range and depth of reference not aroused within the parochial accounts of life in Britain. The same word appears to have different meanings in the two contexts and it is not surprising that newspaper commentators and politicians resist the use of a single term for these very different conditions of life: their indignation at the use of 'poverty' to describe conditions in the UK is not simply a product of their own vested interests (although that is clearly a factor, particularly for many politicians whose decisions are responsible for many of these conditions, such as homelessness in Britain) but also a kind of semantic purity – the boundaries of the term are being preserved and there is a fear that to give legitimacy to referents of a less extreme kind will be to render the term less 'meaningful' and effective.

The crisis in the Sudan and Ethiopia similarly depends on definitions of poverty that include 'starvation' and death as well as on statistics representing the large numbers involved. The photographs in *The Guardian* over the period were mainly of mothers and children, the dominant motif being infants attempting to suckle breasts that had dried up. As a sign for 'poverty' this image plays upon Christian portrayal of the Madonna and Child – the front-page photograph on 1 May figured a mother kneeling with a child sitting on her lap, its head nestled against her breast, in a close replica of the Madonna pose. A *Weekend Guardian* photo-journal account of the 'Crisis in Africa' – this time representing Mozambique – employs a similar photograph with the caption 'Shrinking Baby: Her baby suffered from protein deficiency as Amalia's milk slowly dried up while surviving on a diet of leaves and wild fruit' (see Fig. 2.1). This piece was part of a different genre than the news reporting – that of 'photo-journalism', favoured in colour magazines and weekend supplements, but the imagery and narrative replicate that of the news genre. The drying up of mother's milk becomes an icon for 'poverty' in Third World contexts: that it does not appear in reporting on poverty in the UK both illustrates the discursive choices being made in the media and brings home their emotional effects.

During the same period, *The Guardian* ran a four-page special report entitled 'The forgotten famine' about the food crisis in Africa, fronted by a half-page picture captioned: 'A stomach distended through hunger, a child weak through malnutrition. Warning signals have been flashing imminent famine in Africa since last August' (26.4.91). Similar pictures appear on other pages, one with a caption 'Life at the bottom ... waiting for water in a relief camp at Asmara, Ethiopia. For many the long trek to this camp will end in death as conditions are cramped and squalid and the outbreak of disease is inevitable.' Headlines to articles are couched in warning terms: 'Waiting for the Wave of Death'; 'Pain and Priorities'; 'Born to Die a Slow and Painful Death'. Truth propositions and warning represent the primary discursive strategies and there is little scope for readers to challenge the veracity of the claims or the composition of the photographs, as they were encouraged to do in the UK case.

Nor is this evidence of the relationship between discourses on Third World 'poverty' and those on the UK merely circumstantial – contemporaneous reporting with no necessary linkage – although this alone would be strong support for my suggestion that texts on UK poverty are informed by this wider context. In a number of the reports an explicit contrast is drawn between conditions in the UK and the scenes of death and starvation in the Third World. *The Guardian* (2.5.91) ran a story of a 'Skip Lunch' campaign launched by Save the Children, citing Princess Anne's appeal to people to donate their lunch money to help pay for

SHRINKING BABY: Her baby suffered from protein deficiency as Amalia's breast milk slowly dried up while surviving on a diet of leaves and wild fruit.

Figure 2.1 Photograph reproduced from the *Weekend Guardian* Saturday-Sunday, April 20–21 1991

famine relief. 'The plight of 27 million Africans who face starvation was highlighted when Princess Anne missed lunch and said the money spent on a business meal could feed 450 people in an African village.' The princess said that she was frequently being offered three-course meals that she did not want: 'To counter the excess she suggested that those organising civic or business lunches for her should forget the meal and give the cost to Save the Children': ' "I would be quite happy to forgo a lunch if it meant saving a life", she said.' The message was reinforced by the Minister of Overseas Development, Lynda Chalker, who said: 'It is the public's Christian duty to give money to help starving Africans.' The *Daily Mirror* brought this message home to their readers in more striking fashion, playing upon the same imagery and conveying the same underlying message: comparing distended stomachs in Britain and in the Third World in such a way as to imply that the poverty/affluence associated with such images is an individual moral issue, rather than one of structural economic and political relations. A photograph (in the *Daily Mirror*, 2.5.91) represents Cyril Smith with large stomach thrust forward wearing a tee-shirt labelled 'I skipped lunch', as part of the campaign to raise money for the Save the Children appeal. The story focuses on Smith and his difficulties getting into the tee-shirt because he is so fat, and makes no mention of the substantive issues of poverty and starvation, apart from the campaign slogan: 'skip lunch and save a life'. But the image of the distended stomach is a familiar one in Development and Famine discourse and for many readers the context of this story will have ensured that Smith's stomach and those of the starving children for whom he has skipped lunch will be juxtaposed in a way that makes the moral point about Western affluence and Third World poverty. Third World poverty, then, is not negotiable as accounts of poverty (and of affluence) in the UK are. Rather, they are used as a standard against which those domestic accounts can be judged.

A further comparison with the British meaning of 'poverty' was provided during the period under consideration by the prominent news coverage of the Kurds' retreat into the mountains of Iraq as they escaped the forces of Saddam Hussein, with whom Britain and the United Nations had recently been engaged in war. Harrowing and highly dramatic stories and pictures of people struggling up snowy mountain tracks, sleeping under polythene in freezing temperatures and of children and old people dying in large numbers again set standards for poverty that *Breadline Britain* could not easily compete with even if it wished to. The contrast was compounded in the case of the Kurds by the framing narrative of retreat from a monstrous dictator who had earlier napalmed these same people and was continuing to bomb them.

Again it might seem exceptional that all of this was happening during the period under study but I would suggest that any period in recent years would generate a comparable set of images: whether repeated from periods of high intensity or derived from new 'disasters' they tend to be depicted in the same formulaic style. Not only, then, were there reported major disasters in different parts of the world that called for help from the 'West', during the ten days under investigation, but also the Gulf War was generating its own dramas and desires, its own pictures of helpless victims appealing for Western aid. In the newspapers of the period the American marines and their allies frequently took on the role of saviours, invited in by hapless and starving people fleeing the despotism of Saddam Hussein. A photograph in *The Independent* (24.3.91) shows a group of Iraquis with arms outstretched 'reaching for food' as a Saudi army truck brings supplies. Refugees shelter in tents on mountainsides as relief agencies bring food (*The Independent*, 25.4.93). A devastated landscape is depicted, with piles of rubble and lines of ragged clothes stretched out between trees, above the caption 'Kurdish refugees from Iraq pitch a rough and ready camp' (*The Independent*, 26.4.91). Senior Kurdish leaders appeal to the international community 'to extend an international zone of protection to all of Iraqui Kurdistan' (*The Guardian*, 24.4.91).

Another front-page story of the effects of the Gulf War (*The Guardian*, 29.4.91) depicts two women with children in the now familiar iconic pose, with the caption 'A Kurdish refugee and her mother with her 10-day-old twins . . . They are short of food and the mother cannot give milk.' Again the news stories are replicated in the magazine sections. *The Independent* (27.4.93) for instance ran a story under the ironic heading 'Modern Time: Despair on the Mountain' showing patients at a makeshift outdoor hospital laid out on stretchers on the ground as helpers held drips above them. The scene is directly linked to the familiar theme of humanitarian Western intervention to 'save' the vulnerable peoples of the Third World against the ravages of dictators or of natural catastrophe. The story line opens: 'This was the sort of scene that finally convinced President Bush that for all the legal niceties, for all his fears about getting sucked into a problem he could not get out of, something had to be done for the Kurds.' Since Bush himself never travelled to Iraq the 'scene' referred to here is not the 'real world' one that an observer might encounter on the hillsides of Kurdistan, but the media depiction, framed by photographic selection, caption and heading. By this sleight of hand the newspaper gives itself credit both for representing reality and for influencing presidents. The media 'scene' *is* the actual scene as regards the Western observer. Behind this photo-realism a great deal of ideological work can be done. For instance, the political message that the West was reluctant to enter the political arena – even to save the Kurds – conveniently elides the ways in which the United States and her allies had armed Saddam Hussein in the first place. For present purposes, though, the important point is that this 'scene' further reinforces the notion that 'poverty' in the Third World looks different from the ways it looks in Britain; the term is given a different content, its semantic load is not what it contains in the home context.

Conclusion

The repetition – indeed overdetermination – evident in newspaper images and stories of poverty in the Third World that we have been considering can be interpreted as a sign not so much of the limited repertoire available to reporters as of a homogenizing conceptualization of the Third World itself. Different places, times and causes of poverty (drought, warfare, cyclones, dictators, earthquakes, World Bank economic policy) are rolled up into a few simple messages and texts. This can be seen as a twentieth-century version of those stereotyped novels of Empire (such as those by Rider Haggard, Rudyard Kipling and A. E. Mason) that first acquainted British audiences with non-European society (cf. Street 1975). Then the motifs were of Africa or Asia as 'backward', 'primitive' lands whose politics was either anarchy or despotism, whose religion was simple-minded worship of fearful figures, and whose people were without law and morality. In that genre British travellers were welcomed because they brought civilization and trade: as Lynda Chalker points out a century later, this is their 'Christian duty'. Popular novelists used the exotic landscape and its people as a backcloth against which heroes worked out problems begun at home, so that Africa became a kind of outward bound school for testing the mettle of British men (Street 1985). These nineteenth-century narratives have been brought up to date, according to Busia (1985), by recent adventure stories of the 'buccaneer as liberator' such as those by Frederick Forsyth and Wilbur Smith. The hapless mothers and children who index Third World poverty on the front pages of contemporary newspapers continue to represent appeals for help from the wretched of the earth to these powerful and 'civilized' liberators in the 'developed' world. The new buccaneers – now in the form of US Marines and their allies – have the same state legitimation, the same conceptual apparatus of modern/backward, affluent/rich, civilized/barbarous that underpinned the colonial traveller.

If British identity is constructed to some extent out of such images and in contrast with that 'other' world of poverty and helplessness then no such liberatory mission can appear necessary within Britain itself. Against the representation of the Third World's needs for aid and support, now focused in narratives and images of poverty, stories of homelessness and hardship in the UK can call forth no such sympathy. Media depiction of those sleeping rough in London must appear trivial in comparison: these people can be represented as having it easy, as perverse in making such a 'choice'. Against the dictatorships of Third World society, the British State can be represented as relatively benign in its attitudes to its 'poor' – if such they can be called. In this context, the debate over relative poverty – using indices such as access to telephones, carpets in houses and family holidays – can be made to appear indulgent and obscene. Moreover, this relative poverty becomes associated in media discourse with sham propaganda, taking money for 'acting the part' and political vote-winning. True poverty in contrast, is represented by real people (not actors) in genuine fear of death, and exhibits the harrowing features that justify the familiar headlines – 'Pain', 'Slow Death', 'Misery', 'Millions Starve' – and the 'civilized' intervention. These, I would argue, are the discursive contexts and contrasts that underline the reception of stories about poverty in Britain and against which *Breadline Britain* was set, conceptually if often subconsciously, in its attempt to put poverty back on the agenda in this country. The context in which the programme makers' texts were read to some extent worked against the agenda they were trying to establish.

The case study provided by the media data used here gives some credence to the existence of a connection between discourses on poverty in the UK and those with an international perspective. The methodological approach adopted in this volume towards text and context has, I would argue, allowed that connection to be made visible where it might otherwise be ineluctable. Other methodologies can now be helpfully employed to elaborate and test the argument further – statistical surveys of viewer response; ethnographic interviews with a wide range of viewers; ethnographic study of those actually living in poverty. One feature of the approach adopted in this volume is that it does not claim to be comprehensive but rather to provide a generative and interdisciplinary way of opening up fields previously restricted by the narrowness of disciplinary boundaries.

The methodology employed here with respect to questions of poverty can also be used to open up new questions on other subjects. In a sense the main subject of this chapter (and of the volume as a whole) is not poverty itself or even representations of poverty – but the question of how we approach text. Where that has previously seemed the province of textual linguistics or of literary criticism, we would argue that it requires a broader-based approach that can handle not only the immediate analysis of text but the enveloping levels of context that give it meaning. If this chapter has made some contribution to that case then it will have succeeded in its primary aim.

References

Busia, A. (1985) Manipulating Africa: the buccaneer as 'liberator' in contemporary fiction. In Dabydeen, D. (ed.) *The Black Presence in English Literature*. Manchester: Manchester University Press.

Coates, K. and Silburn, J. (1970) *Poverty: The Forgotten Englishman*. London: Penguin.

Fairclough, N. (1985) Critical and Descriptive Goals in Discourse Analysis. *Journal of Pragmatics,* 9: 739–63.

Goldthorpe, J. (1969) *The Affluent Worker and the Class Structure*. Cambridge: Cambridge University Press.

Goldthorpe, J. et al. (1980) *Social Mobility and Class Structure*. Oxford: Clarendon Press.

Lockwood, D. et al. (1958) *The Blackcoated Worker*, London: Allen & Unwin.

Mackenzie, J. (ed.) (1986) *Imperialism and Popular Culture*. Manchester: Manchester University Press.

Mitchell, C. (1984) Typicality and the case study. In Ellen, R. (ed.) *Ethnographic Research: A Guide to General Conduct*. London: Academic Press.

Street, B. (1975) *The Savage in Literature*. London: Routledge & Kegan Paul.

Street, B. (1985) Reading the novels of empire: race and ideology in the classic 'tale of adventure'. In Dabydeen, D. (ed.) *The Black Presence in English Literature*. Manchester: Manchester University Press.

Townsend, P. (1979) *Poverty in the United Kingdom: A Survey of Household Resources and Standards of Living.* London: Penguin.

Westergaard, J. (1972) The myth of classlessness. In Blackburn, R. (ed.) *Ideology in Social Science.* London: Fontana, pp. 130–3.

3 *From the street to the screen:* Breadline Britain *and the semiotics of poverty*

Ulrike Meinhof

> We are not concerned with the very poor. They are unthinkable, and only to be approached by the statistician or the poet.
> (E. M. Forster, *Howards End*, 1910: 44)

The narrator in E. M. Forster's novel *Howards End* marks with this observation the boundary between the relative poverty and deprivation of the character Leonard Bast and another, unthinkable kind of poverty which is no longer within reach of either himself, nor the other characters in the novel: the genteel, middle- and upper middle-class English liberals of the (Bloomsbury derived) circle of the Schlegel sisters, and the rich upcoming coarse new business class represented through the Wilcox family.

The question of whether and how the social plight of a section of our population can, is, or should be represented is not specific to the novelist's concern, nor to other forms of fictional representation on television or film. Any form of the news and documentary media, from newspaper reports to television documentaries, reports, narrates and represents people and events involving social concerns, and, by doing so, generates further discourses. These may be in the media themselves, where programmes about programmes, and intertextual references to other media texts have become standard practice.[1] Or they may be outside the media, in the full spectrum of public and private domains; from political speeches quoting or challenging a particular programme to the reactions, narrations and discussions of viewers and readers.[2] The focus of this chapter and that by Kay Richardson in this volume is on such discourses and representations of poverty, and how they interact with each other. As main example I have chosen *Breadline Britain* (from now on referred to in this chapter as *BB*), a series about poverty in the UK which coincided in two of its six parts with the period of our media search, in particular programme 1 (the definition of poverty) and programme 4 (the programme dealing with housing and homelessness).

Three different, though interconnected, perspectives will be discussed:

1. The interaction between the discourse of the social scientists alias programme makers about how to draw a poverty line, and the representation of this in televisual form.
2. The interplay between the different semiotic codes or levels of these representations, namely the interaction of words, images, and music.
3. The intervention of critical readings of these representations, in our case specifically those of *The Media Show*, and the problems this raises.

The analysis will be guided by a form of 'social semiotics', which means in the words of Halliday, 'interpreting language within a sociocultural context, in which the culture itself is interpreted in semiotic terms – as an information system . . .' (Halliday 1978: 2). In the following brief section I want to explain what kind of methodology this implies and how it differs from other approaches to discourse.

Why social semiotics?

An interest in discourse means coming to terms with the vexed question of whether any of the many different theories of discourse can throw light on the problems raised by the interacting and conflicting discourses involving *BB*, and if so, how. The validity of a *theory* of discourse for our discourse analysis will thus be assessed by its effectiveness as an interpretative tool. Testing a theory by methods or practices derived from it is not the only, for some not even an important, part of the contribution which a theory has to make. However, for the purposes of a discourse *analysis* it is essential that the underlying principles of the approach are understood and their relationship to existing theories clarified, and, if possible, enhanced.

The first question to be addressed in this chapter is thus: What makes a social semiotic approach to discourse distinctive? Or in other words: Is there a difference between what social semiotics sees as its object of enquiry, and thus in the methodology which guides the enquiry and analysis and other approaches to discourse? To answer this I will draw two lines of demarcation against two competing theories of discourse which in spite of considerable overlap with social semiotics in some areas are nevertheless substantially and significantly different in others: semiotics proper on the one hand, and postmodernist/poststructuralist approaches to discourse on the other.

Semiotics and social semiotics meet in that they view all texts as communication, as 'information systems', to use Halliday's phrase (Halliday 1978: 2). 'Text' in semiotics does not restrict itself to the spoken and written words but also, most importantly, includes all the other semiotic ways of encoding meaning, such as architecture, fashion, kinship systems, traffic signs, to name but a few. In the context of our television series a semiotic analysis would be bound to include an analysis of the images and the music used in the programmes and thus differ substantially from a linguistic or sociolinguistic approach which would only capture the verbal part of the communication. But my perspective in this chapter is not just semiotic, but forms part of a *social* semiotic. This means that whereas in semiotics the sign is taken to be independent from its context, and meaning is established by its opposition to other signs inside a closed system of signification, social semiotics in particular explores the correspondence and interconnection between social practices and discourse. For the purposes of our analysis of the *BB* series, this has two implications: first, an exploration of the nature of the *context* in which the programmes were made to show how a particular view of social reality was constructed and then translated into the sequences of the television series; and secondly, in response to this, an account of the *interaction* of the different codes which are supposed to realize interdependently this construction. Each code is thus not taken as a separate system of meaning, but as interrelating. Insofar as my analysis of *BB* suggests an interpretation of the interplay between image and sound, which favours a particular view or interpretation of social reality, this resembles a kind of textual reading which I have elsewhere referred to as 'closed'[3] (Meinhof 1993: 213), and which is a familiar way of applying social semiotic theory to the interpretation of texts in context. But this is not sufficient. The view of social semiotics adopted here is one which has profited not only from the seminal study by Michael Halliday which made it possible to theorize the interconnection between text and social structure; it has equally been influenced by Volosinov's and Bakhtin's notion of the 'dialogic': a dynamic, interactive view of discourse as arising between socially organized individuals, where contestation is part of any discourse (Volosinov 1973; Bakhtin 1981). Social semiotics then takes the old semiotic path from sender to message to receiver (Jakobson 1960) and explodes it into multidimensional interactive sets of relations. As a result, the meaning of discourse ceases to coincide with the interpretation of its textual strategies, relegating such readings to that of an 'implied reader'. Closed textual analysis of fixed signs with fixed meanings is opened up to and thus superseded by contestation and polyphony of meaning at every point of the semiotic interactions, including the multiple readings of actual viewers with different experiential backgrounds, attitudes and feelings. In this chapter the contestation of a dominant reading will be illustrated by reference to a particular controversy arising from the clash between the discourse of homelessness in programme 4 and an alternative discourse offered by *The Media Show*; that is a contestation within related televisual genres. Richardson in the following chapter will move the issue of contestation away from the 'intertelevisual' domains by an analysis of the responses of different groups of viewers. To get a full account of the different interactive processes, this chapter and that of Richardson should be taken as complementary.

Surrendering the text as a unitary concept, or relegating its authorial inflection to one among many possible readings, is not a new phenomenon, but one that is familiar since the postmodernist deconstruction of the single text with a proprietorial author. The second line of demarcation for a distinctive social semiotic approach to discourse is thus that against some forms of postmodernism. Whereas the insistence on multiple readings and polyphony is a shared concern with postmodernism, and, as

Richardson rightly points out, almost commonplace in terms of how one conducts television audience research, there is nevertheless a crucial difference, especially against the more extreme forms of postmodernism, which will become clear in my discussion of the quarrel between *BB* and *The Media Show* over the validity of *BB*'s representation of homelessness. My insistence on polyphony of meaning is not a denial of potential and actual constraints on interpretation; nor am I claiming that a text has as many meanings as there are readers. There is, to answer Fish's provocative title-question, very definitely 'a text in this class' (Fish 1980). It is precisely the interplay and tension between the different kinds of meaning we have already discussed in our introduction: between the making of meaning in the making of text, and in the remaking of text in the readings.

To establish this interplay we need first of all to turn to the way the programme makers arrived at their definition of poverty.

What is poverty? *Breadline Britain* and its construction of poverty

Breadline Britain is based on a Mori survey of 1,800 people commissioned by the programme makers themselves, to investigate the attitude of British people, about what in 1990 constitutes an unacceptably low standard of living. In the survey people were asked to indicate on a list of items which of those they felt to be essential. Items which more than 50 per cent of the sample listed as such were then taken into account in the definition of poverty applying the following formula: if anyone lacks three or more of these 'essential' items this is taken as an indication of deprivation. In applying this definition of poverty to the British population as a whole, the researchers discovered that in 1990 11 million people in Britain are poor. (This figure of 11 million compares to 7.5 million in 1983, when *BB* conducted its first survey for an earlier series along the same lines: an increase of 3.5 million in seven years) The definition of poverty is thus related to lacking 'essentials' which a majority of British people feel that no-one should be without. Such a list includes, for example, a damp-free house (specified by 98 per cent as essential), an inside toilet, not shared with another household (97 per cent), and beds for everyone in the household (95 per cent); it also, more controversially, includes items which in 1983 were not felt to be necessities by more than 50 per cent of the sample population, but which in 1990 are, such as a telephone (56 per cent), an outing for children once a week (53 per cent), and having children's friends round for tea/snack fortnightly (52 per cent). Poverty is thus not a question of physical survival, although the detrimental effect of poverty on health has been established through epidemiological research (see Wilkinson 1990), and is directly addressed by the programmes; nor is it simply related to income distribution (i.e. people living on less than 50 per cent of the average national income count as poor), though people who lack such items are heavily concentrated among those with the lowest income.[4] Poverty and deprivation in *BB* are consensual definitions which shift in line with the relative expectations of society as a whole.

The number of poor in the UK which was thus established, is not a propagandist distortion, as was alleged by some of the hostile press reports.[5] It is, in fact, in line with that recorded by other studies, such as the most recent one by the European Commission on relative poverty levels in the EC.[6] But in its emphasis on what the British population feels about the bare necessities of life in 1990, it provides a highly tangible form of translating an abstract notion such as a poverty line into concrete instances of deprivation. This, of course, does not guarantee that viewers of *BB* will follow and accept the logic by which 'the poor' are identified, as will be shown in Richardson's discussion of audience responses to the programme. Indeed, the difference in viewer responses to this theoretical thesis-like construction of poverty in contrast to their relating to the images of individual poor people portrayed by the programme is one of the points discussed there.

The semiotic organization of *Breadline Britain*

The makers of *BB* chose the format of the documentary[7] to present their arguments about poverty in the UK. The choice of the documentary genre is not an automatic one, since television has other, frequently more popular, means of presenting a view of social reality. The much debated and highly influential television drama, *Cathy Come Home* (hereafter *CCH*), from 1966, directed by Kenneth Loach, was a fictional story, involving a script writer (Jeremy Sandford), a film producer (Tony Garnett), and actors

(Carol White as Cathy and Ray Brooks as Reg). Clearly marked as television drama *CCH* was nevertheless accepted by a deeply moved mass audience as a convincing account of the situation in the UK at the time, with some consequences for the public sphere of social policy-making. Jeremy Sandford, in his introduction to the publication of his screenplay, wrote in 1976:

> I wish that there had been more change in the general situation of Britain's homeless since I wrote *Cathy*. As regards its particular effect, however, I can feel pleased. It is good to know that I have altered, if only by a very small bit, the condition of life for others in my own society. As a result of the film and certain meetings we held in Birmingham afterwards, this town, and others, ceased their practice of separating three or four hundred husbands each year from their wives and children (Sandford 1976: 14).

Dramatizations which use fictional accounts and actors to represent a particular view of social reality or figures in public life are regular features on television, with a frequent mixing of formats which often blurs the dividing line between fictional and non-fictional accounts. So-called 'factions', in particular, often mix genres by combining apparently authentic acted reconstructions of particular historical moments with genuine newsreels and other documentary material from the archives. Critical comment, too, is often favouring fictions or drama documentaries, praising reconstructions and dramatized versions as more convincing and more genuine renderings of past events than eyewitness accounts.[8] For viewers, then, the dividing line between fictional and non-fictional representation, and their respective relationship to social reality is not necessarily as clearcut and as obvious as generic descriptions seem to imply.

The makers of *BB*, however, chose the documentary format and, in keeping with its generic conventions, selected ordinary people rather than actors to talk about their lives and living conditions.

The following extract is taken from the beginning of the soundtrack of programme 1 of *BB* and introduces six individuals who reappear right through the series together with some others, and who each represent a particular aspect or aspects of poverty as defined through the criteria explained in section 1 of this chapter.

1(a)

Robert's room here. There's only one bed. One wardrobe. No carpets at all, curtains are second hand. As we go into the daughter's room. As you can see: one chest of drawers. Very little carpet, again. As you can see, it's absolutely bare. (Richard Winers, programme 1)

1(b)

I always have to do the washing in the bathroom with the shower water. Because I can't afford the launderette, because the cost of the washerette is astronomical. You can't possibly afford it on pension. I have a 50p meter because I couldn't afford a big electricity bill. When the 50p is gone the meter just clicks off and you haven't got another one. You just go to bed. There's no light, and no heat, and there's no water. (Julie Smith, 77 year-old widow, programme 1)

1(c)

As you can see in the bedroom, you've got a build up of condensation. You can actually see how damp it is. Sometimes the window is actually very wet, and you got the curtain sticking to the window. In the toilet you get a lot of condensation. You get water dripping off the window. You got a lot of fungus, plus the wallpaper is lifting off. In the winter it's very very cold. (Yvonne Barnett, programme 1)

1(d)

I got my cooker off the rag and bone man, and I got it for free. I think the cooker is definitely dangerous, I mean. I'll be out for most of the day, come back in and it stinks. But I can't ring the Gas Board, because if I do they come down on the cooker and I won't be able to use it and I can't cook my meals. (John Malone, programme 1)

1(e)

<'Let's try to come down, hey. O.K.'>
Before Jimmy had the accident and he was working, we could afford most things, but now, on the money we're on, you can't go out and buy what you need. It's a case of like, going into debt and get them, or doing without. And most of the time you have to do without. (Wife of disabled man, Jimmy Roberts, programme 1)

1(f)

Basically if I can't pay and I haven't got money from the Social, whatever, that means I can't buy it . . . that is nothing to eat.

It's not like Oliver Twist knocking on people's door and say 'can I have some more porridge', because they're just going to kick you out. <'Can you spare any change, please?'>
(Kim Stevens, programme 1)

Each instance stands in for a particular group of people living in poverty, as defined by the researchers on the basis of the Mori survey. Programme 1 of the series elucidates this by taking each of six clusters in turn: housing and heating; food; clothing; furniture; leisure and social activities; financial security. Each of these clusters is personified by particular individuals who are illustrating a particular category of lack and deprivation, which is then related back to the attitude of the British people that these items are essential for living. The programme ranges from the most destitute – a girl living in the street – to those who are at first sight not as dramatically poor – a disabled man forced to live with his parents again, or a young man with a broken cooker. What they are all lacking are three or more of the key items which people in the Britain of 1990 felt no-one should go without. The programme makes it clear right from the start that its case studies have been carefully selected in relation to the clusters of relative deprivation established in the survey. The 'representational' function of the people concerned is thus a crucial and undisguised element of the programme's textual organization. The seven individuals or households to which we return throughout the series stand in for the vast and, since 1983, growing number of poor people in the UK.

At the end of each sequence a voice-over explains the rationale of the programme in exactly the terms I have just given you.

This six part series is about the poor in Britain today. It updates a similar series of *BB* made in 1983. Amidst the growing affluence of the 1980s, how have the poor fared? These families lack the things that most of us take for granted. But is there a living standard unacceptably low for the 1990s? Are they poor? The first question is: where do we draw the poverty line?

Once poverty was seen to be just about physical survival. Now it's accepted that a minimal standard should allow for more than this. So what are the necessities that no-one should go without? This is ultimately a matter for the judgement of the society at large. We commissioned a survey of 1,800 people. They were asked which of a wide range of items are essential for a minimal living standard and which everyone should be able to afford. (Voice-over, programme 1)

The voice belongs to Charlotte Cornwell, who was hired for

this purpose, and it is her voice that relates throughout the series each instance shown to the general thesis: that poverty is relative to the expectations of society as a whole, that it exists and has worsened in Britain during the last decade, and that changes in government policy have directly contributed to this increase in the number of the poor.

Explicitness about its thesis is thus one of the marked organizational principles of the series, with the voice-over acting as the medium for setting out the argument, and introducing each instance as part of that argument. Although television documentaries usually rely on voice-overs to interpret the instances they show, the insistence in *BB* on which particular aspect of poverty each group is representing, and how this relates to the general research findings, is unusual, and gives the series a more academic perspective than others of the same genre.

But how are the people themselves presented? Again, documentary filming has explored different options to cope with the fact that the presence of a camera or an observer will affect and alter the way people behave, from fly-on-the-wall positions which seem to suggest that the camera is not really there, to films which show cameras and camera crew, interviewer and interviewee as part of the same scene. *BB* adopted an intermediate position for most of the series. There are very few 'fly-on-the-wall', naturalistic settings, although there are some (not very successful) sequences where people are involved in make-believe encounters with officials, or just going about their daily lives as if the camera was not present. The quotes 1(a) to 1(f) illustrate this. In terms of tenor-relations[9] the addressee of the speakers is rarely another person shown on screen, or if so, as in the first line of 1(e) and the last line of 1(f), only very briefly, acting more as introduction of the clip or as transition to the next. This has consequences both for the language the speakers use and for the interaction between camera and speaker/image and text. Most often the speakers appear to be directly telling of their plight, on camera and sometimes in voice-over. No interviewer appears on screen and no questions are heard off-camera. The interviewer's role has been effaced and the subjects appear to be setting their own agenda.

The absence of an addressee in the film does not imply a foregrounding of the camera as a device, which is one of the suggestions from postmodern theory for defeating the pitfalls of realism.[10] Its role is left implicit, though its existence is not repressed as is the role of the interviewer. Most of the comments of the people on the screen are done in their own voice-over, as in extract 1(a) above.

Here Richard Winers explains that he and his family have no money to buy furniture as he is shown, on screen, to be walking into an empty room. The sentences are extremely brief referring directly to items of his immediate physical environment: room, bed, wardrobe, no carpets, and so on. The labelling of these items happens while the hand-held camera pans around the room to show the bed in the corner, the empty floor, the lamp on the floor with a bare bulb and so on. When Richard moves between rooms, the camera follows, keeping him in shot. The cuts are few, and do not elide real time and space.

Very interesting in view of the absent addressee is the frequent use of phrases like 'as you can see', or similar formulations (see in particular 1(a) and 1(c) above which appear like a direct reference to an unseen camera taking its lead from the speaker. Yvonne Barnet, the single mother of three children who all sleep in one room and share one bed in 1(c) uses the same phrase as Richard, 'as you can see', to draw the camera's attention to the dripping windows and the damp walls, picking up pieces of wet wallpaper and drops of water between her fingers as she speaks.

The camera is thus very much in the role of the eye-witness, seemingly acting on behalf of the individuals telling their own story.

The images suggest that what people say about their lives is, indeed, correct. The people describe what they have to do, as they are doing it, they talk about their living conditions, as they point to the broken stove, or the damp window and the camera follows their gaze. There is thus very often a complete overlap between text and picture, a total mutual reinforcement of sound and vision. This overlap is interesting since it differs as a technique from that more widely used in film reports on television news and television documentary, where the relationship between the aural and visual is often either one of displacement or dichotomy.[11] It enforces the sense of total authenticity of the narratives of each individual. The narrator's voice-over at the end of each section does not need to *interpret* these narratives – this is done by the people themselves – her comments incorporate the individual instances into the general thesis.

The representational techniques of programme 1 reappear in programme 4 – 'No place like home'. Statistical figures and observations about the housing situation in Britain are illustrated through the instances of the three women in the programme: Alison, a single mother forced to live with her son in bed and breakfast accommodation; a 17 year-old homeless girl, Kim (see also extract 1(f) above) and Yvonne, a single mother of three who lives in a run-down council estate (see also extract 1(c)).

The following quotes come from the opening sequences of programme 4, and again introduce each individual by letting them speak directly to the camera, though again there are very brief sequences where the interaction is between the people shown, such as the opening remark of Alison talking to her baby.

Some extracts from programme 4:

4(a) *Alison to her baby son*: <'No, come and do a wee wee . . .'>
This is my seventh month. It's just horrible. I've got no privacy, nor has he. If he's like, misbehaving, I've got nowhere I can go on my own, he's got nowhere he can go. And how I'm living it's just degrading to think that I have to live like this before I could get my flat from the Council. Otherwise they won't give me a flat.

Voice-over: Alison Child is 21. With no home of her own she lives with her two-and-a-half year-old son Ricki in this Bed and Breakfast hotel in Bayswater in London.

Alison: He doesn't want sharing. He's backwards in his talking, and he is just very hyperactive. If he had more children to play with, because he'd get rid of all that energy, he's got. Like, he just can't he's got so much of it.

4(b)
Kim (seen sitting on the street): It's quite dangerous sleeping out in the street. There's some weird people around, you know. I mean when you're freezing cold, and you really are cold, and you're shaking, and someone comes up and asks you for a cup of coffee and you can stay at his house, and you can sit in his car for a while. Perverts, like, take advantage of you especially if you're homeless, you know what I'm saying, and they give you money and then ask you to do them favours, and things like that.

Voice-over: Kim Stevens is 17. Brought up in care, she's been sleeping rough in London for two years.

Kim (voice blends in slowly with camera focusing on people lying on the floor underneath blankets): Sleeping rough is really difficult. We used to sleep up Deans Street, and three car parks we slept in, and we got moved on from each one. Where we sleep, sometimes especially on the West End side, you sit down somewhere and they move you on before you even have your sleeping bag out. But if you're sleeping out, sometimes they wake you up, about three in the morning and then six, you hardly get any sleep. And especially when you're nice and warm in your sleeping bag, you're cuddling up in your sleeping bag and you're nice and warm. They come and kick you in the ribs, and tell you to get up, and you get all cold and wet again.

After this introduction the voice-over connects their individual narratives to the government's changes in housing policy, such as the selling off of council property, the lifting of rent controls, the withdrawal of benefits to 16 and 17 year-olds, to the lack of adequate or, indeed, absence of any housing facilities for people on low income.

These are among the 11 million people found to be in poverty by a special survey commissioned for *Breadline Britain*. They all fall below the minimum living standard laid down by society at large. This is a rise of 3½ million since the first *Breadline Britain* survey in 1983. This found a third of those in poverty had housing problems. Since then government housing policy has radically changed. So what effect has this had on the housing of the poor? (Voice-over, programme 4)

Again, the representational nature of each selected individual is stressed, from the most destitute, Kim, who lives on the streets of London, to Alison who simply has not got a home of her own, but who is at least in a warm room in her bed and breakfast accommodation, and Yvonne Barnett, whose flat is damp and in an unsightly and dirty housing block. Ranging across all three narratives reinforces once more the sense of the relativity of poverty in the UK, in contrast to the absolute poverty familiar from Third World images of malnutrition and starvation. The consensus view of the British public as established by the survey, states that Alison and Yvonne with their children, and not just the homeless Kim, live in totally inadequate conditions: they, too, are poor. This is particularly interesting in the light of the highly critical comments made by *The Media Show* which will be discussed in the final section of this chapter.

Breadline Britain and the melancholia of poverty

Apart from the different voices and different images of *BB*, there is a third semiotic layer which, in an unobtrusive way, interprets the situation of the poor in the UK: the music of the opening and closing credit sequences of each programme in the series.

In these, the camera is moving across scenes and people's faces, who are featured in the series. The images blend in and out of each other, individual faces appear as the camera pans the landscape, and each scene changes to the next without an obvious cut or transition as the faces fade away. The opening sequence begins with an industrial landscape: the smoking industrial chimneys of IBM, superimposed on which the face of a young man appears. As he is blended out, the camera moves to the tower block of a Birmingham housing estate, with the face of an older man moving across it. Next is a view of Merseyside with the face of a young woman with a child, followed by a street scene with homeless youngsters sleeping on the ground; and finally, we move from the face of a young woman to the inside of a bare room, with the face of an old man in the foreground. The sequence closes on a cracked window pane. In both, the opening and the slightly different ending sequence, the backgrounds are shot in a bluish tinted black and white which gives the film a grainy look; the faces of the people who are superimposed on these backgrounds are in grey; the look is one of great solemnity. Accompanying these images are the gentle sounds of a piano which plays an extremely simple, almost amateurish string of sounds, which lack a distinct melody and a strong foregrounded theme. Instead it is vague and wandering, a sense which the consistent use of the pedal and the consequent tonal blurring reinforces. There are twelve bars altogether:

Gm Gm F F
Cm E^b Gm Gm
Dm E^b Gm Gm

Such a transition from E flat major (E^b) to G minor (Gm) is not only an age-old archetype of European music connoting sadness and despair, most notably in Chopin's *Funeral March*; it similarly appears in dozens of popular songs which decry a hopeless destiny. Philip Tagg (1993: 66–73)[12] identified a list which includes among others such different songs and styles as that of Dylan's 'All along the watch-tower', Pink Floyd's 'Money', Phil Collins's 'In the Air Tonight', and 'Dead End Street' by the Kinks. The music thus reinforces the sad and depressing nature of the images, the strong connotation that here are people resigned to their fate, and that their melancholia is a private, internalized feeling of anguish rather than one of anger at social injustice and rebellion.

To summarize the argument so far:

1. *Breadline Britain* has a thesis based on social science research relating to the poor living conditions of an increasing number of people in Britain.
2. The thesis is exemplified in the programmes through representative instances, that is through individuals whose living conditions are supposed to match the different kinds of deprivation established by the research.
3. These individuals tell their story for the programme with the help of a camera that authenticates their narratives by showing us the relevant images referred to by the speakers. The stories range from the most destitute (homeless people living on the street) to those living under impoverished but not destitute conditions, but they are similar in the tone of sadness and depression. The mood of these narratives is reinforced by the music of the credit sequences which stresses the melancholia of poverty rather than any more aggressive moods.
4. The individual narratives are related back to the general thesis by a separate commentator who is never on camera but speaks in voice-over at the beginning and end of each section. These comments are given in a descriptive and analytical form associated with an academic 'objective' style of reporting rather than any more arousing alternative.

Such a differentiation between the discourses of individuals and their plight, and the discourse of the general thesis, the claim that these are instances of the plight of millions of other British people is not at all unusual in the making of documentary fiction: it is one of the obvious means of blending the specific and the general into each other. What is more unusual in the structure of *BB*, though, is the total *separation* between these two discourses, which raises the question of how an audience reacts to these different appeals of credibility. In the response of the audience, which is reported in the next chapter, Richardson found an interesting disparity in what viewers were taking as true and what they were not accepting as accurate reflections of social reality. This is extremely interesting in that the viewers' response seems to reflect the difference in the construction of the programme, yet one would not wish to claim uncritically that their different reaction is an effect of the programme's structure. It is clearly not enough to address the question of how programmes make their meanings by a detailed analysis of the semiotic codes employed such as the one I have just given. A much wider frame of reference is needed which incorporates the viewers' own world knowledge and world views which is the point of Richardson's analysis in Chapter 4.

In the final section of this chapter I want to discuss another reading of the text, that presented by an episode of another television series: *The Media Show*.[13]

Breadline Britain and *The Media Show*: whose poor are telling the truer story?

The quality of the home features on top of the list of items which British people in the Mori survey had felt to be essential for anyone. Inadequate housing or, worse still, the absence of any home for many British people is thus a particularly strong indicator of poverty, and the images shown in programme 4 are among the starkest in the series, in particular those relating to the homeless young people sleeping rough in the streets of London.

The sequences where Kim (called Cathy in *The Media Show*) is seen bedding down in the street together with some of her friends were picked up and critically commented on by Channel 4's *Media Show*. Broadcast in advance of the actual showing of the *BB* series and its housing episode on BBC2, the programme on *The Media Show* discussed the representation of the poor in various television genres, from news programmes to soap operas, but was particularly critical of the ways in which news and current affairs broadcasting deal with the poor.

In the usual style of *The Media Show* the programme accumulated arguments by adding Emma Freud's own analysis to a mixture of clips from interviews with broadcasters, journalists, academics, media analysts, which were, in turn, intercut with film clips from the programmes they discussed and criticized. Among these were the following types of remarks:

1. These programmes are guilty of stereotyping the poor (Chris Pond, Patrick Stoddard).
2. They are always opting for the worst possible cases rather than the typical; they are not giving the poor the opportunity to show themselves in the best possible light; they are always showing the poor as victims (Beatrix Campbell).
3. These programmes are infringing the privacy of the poor and thus deprive them of their dignity (Beatrix Campbell).
4. Programme makers merely slot the poor into narratives that they have pre-defined (Beatrix Campbell); they are not really letting the poor tell their own story.
5. People selected for television are simply playing up to the cameras, and are giving the film makers the version they wish to hear; television thus allows people to perpetuate 'myths about themselves' (Boyce).

Intercut with these comments were clips from news and documentary programmes, with one entire section devoted to the making of *BB* which included interviews with one of the programme makers, Stuart Lansley, and with the homeless young people who were featured in the *BB* series.

The technique of montage adopted by *The Media Show* makes for gripping television, and many of the points made by the interviewees are a necessary reminder of the problematic relationship between the media and its subjects. But there are problems. The way in which the views of different interviewees are accumulated, cut and recast in a new argumentative context, namely that of *The Media Show*'s own, allows that potentially contradictory positions can be stated side by side without the viewers necessarily becoming aware of the fact that such views are not compatible. At the same time an argument can be constructed by cutting statements of interviewees against each other in apparent contradiction, even where these may be perfectly compatible in a different context.

To give just one example: in one clip Polly Toynbee, the Social Affairs Editor from BBC TV, argues in favour of finding a case which most dramatically illustrates a particular situation; after that the journalist/writer Beatrix Campbell is featured as saying the following:

> There is a notion of what you do is to find the worst possible example you can think of, rather than you find examples that exemplify ordinary, typical, everyday poverty. Now ordinary poverty isn't absolutely underesourced. It isn't . . . out on the street, it isn't without furniture, it isn't without, it is with very little. And the difference between being without and with very little is very crucial. Because millions of people live with very little, very few people live with nothing at all.

This is clearly a denial of Polly Toynbee's position. At the same time, though, these comments appear in relation to the critical review of the *BB* programme, which by featuring homeless people in the street seems to be falling into the same trap as that criticized by Beatrix Campbell. Yet it was *The Media Show* itself which, in its concentration on the most dramatic case of poverty in all six programmes of the series, misrepresented the direction which *BB* explicitly adopted and which has been discussed extensively in the first part of this chapter. In *The Media Show*'s representation of *BB* there is no acknowledgement that all its six programmes precisely aim to represent the full range in which poverty manifests itself, from the most deprived, such as homeless Kim, to those who cannot afford a holiday or the launderette. In the very centre of the *BB* thesis is that which Beatrix Campbell asks for, an acknowledgement of poverty as a status relative to the expectations of society as a whole. Only through *The Media Show*'s own selection of the most dramatic case out of a whole range of different ones is this criticism seemingly validated. Yet when Beatrix Campbell is featured again, this time in direct opposition to the *BB* producer Stuart Lansley, she blames programme makers for using the poor to illustrate 'a story that is already completely defined'. But, as Stuart Lansley argues, the 'story' is defined by a consensus view of what constitutes poverty, not by the over-dramatization of individual cases. There is little doubt that in a different argumentative context Beatrix Campbell would agree with the positions taken up by *BB*.

However, the extract from *BB*, and *The Media Show*'s own version of the events, raise another issue. The instance shown in programme 4 of *BB*, where Kim and her friends are bedding down in the street is not literally the moment of the people going to sleep in a doorway, as one would assume from watching the programme, but is a moment created for television. Although there is no doubt that Kim and her friends are genuinely homeless, *The Media Show* 'discovered' some facts about them which they considered problematical, namely that Kim had already featured on three previous television programmes about homelessness, and had in the words of Emma Freud 'reached celebrity' through television. And that the young boys who were featured going to sleep on the street on that night were actually sleeping in hostels.

The following transcript is taken from a part of *The Media Show* which introduces the *BB* series by a fictional 'presenter' who supposedly advises on what it is that documentary film-makers really want. His sarcastic style contrasts with the more factual and analytic one of *The Media Show*'s own moderator, Emma Freud.

Presenter (in studio, supposedly addressing those who are about to be filmed): Remember, they (i.e. the documentary film-makers) are on your side, they've done their research, and they are educated people. Give them what they want; and if you're smart you give them just a little bit more.

Tommo and Michael (talking to The Media Show *about being filmed for BB)*: We stood outside Centrepoint at Deans Street, and Cathy [sic] was there with this lady from the *Breadline* programme. And we just stood there, we just sort of asked if we could be in it, you know we just asked, and we were in.

Emma Freud (voice-over to pictures of BB *editing suite)*: London Weekend Television's major new series *Breadline Britain* will look at what's happening to poverty in the UK through the lives of today's poor.

(Extract with Tommo and Michael shown on editing machine; they talk about how government has not done anything for them, how cold they were; editors of BB *comment and cut)*
Tommo and Michael (in The Media Show *studio).*
Michael: Well I chose the set myself, actually, because I was quite enthusiastic about the whole affair; and we went to this place just off Soho Square, and we chose a nice little alcove where we could sit and

look really miserable. And we had blankets over us. *(Film shows this sequence with his voice in voice-over)*

Tommo: For about five minutes he *(the film producer?)* was telling us, like, you two sit up and chat, and me I was lying down, trying to get some sleep, and they're chatting, and I'm supposed to be shouting out, you two shut up, cause I'm trying to get some sleep. You know, some things just don't happen, you never find three lads in a door way, and then two girls come up; it never happens.

Interviewer's voice: Where were you actually sleeping that night?

Tommo: In a hostel.

Michael: Yeah, I was in a hostel as well.

Tommo: Actually, in a hostel.

(Sequence with Stuart Lansley's comment about his criteria for choosing people; Boyce comments that people perpetuate myths about themselves)
Emma Freud: Since this programme was completed the makers of *Breadline Britain* have issued a statement denying that they were misled by the young people they filmed. They say that these individuals regularly spent the night together on the street, and that as far as they were concerned it makes no difference to them if Michael and Tommo spend the night in a hostel, since most homeless youngsters stay in hostels from time to time. It's widespread practice for TV documentaries to try to find typical examples to illustrate an argument but what can be overlooked in the process are the awkward realities of everyday life. *The Media Show* has confirmed that on the night when they were pretending to sleep rough for the cameras and on subsequent nights Michael and Tommo were definitely staying in a hostel.

This critique raises two fundamental issues. First, that in response to the camera something can be created which otherwise would not exist. This does not concern us here. The poor in Britain clearly exist irrespective of the presence or absence of a camera whatever criteria for defining poverty are used.

The second point is more complicated, and concerns only the realm of representation. Does it matter if a seemingly authentic instance is a dramatized representation which may at this particular moment not account for the actual event as happening there and then, but which is nevertheless an acceptable signal of a particular aspect of social reality; that is if the relationship between the instance and what it stands for is exclusively symbolic? Issue 1 and with it the *thesis* of *BB* is not affected by whether or not the particular people they picked are material instances of what they are representing. If on that particular night the boys slept in the hostel, that does not devalue the fact that many other young people that night, and, indeed, the boys themselves on many other nights were sleeping in the streets, and that homelessness and bad housing in the UK is a central problem for a growing number of poor. *The Media Show* leans heavily on the fact that they 'found out' what the boys were really doing that night. Their attack on *BB* does, however, smack of naive literalism, as when Emma Freud claims in her introduction, that *The Media Show* wants 'to reveal the tricks of the trade ... and let the poor tell *their side* of the story' (my emphasis). How can *The Media Show* be anything but an alternative version of what they themselves criticize when they show us the boys in their bravado in front of the camera of *The Media Show*, or Kim proudly joking about saving up for America. Stories and narratives are obviously being created, narrated and dramatized for television, and this is as much the case for the meta-documentary as it is for the documentary. *The Media Show*'s critique at this point confuses verisimilitude with authenticity.

Although *The Media Show* is to blame for trapping itself in a rather simplistic view of unmediated reality, this does not mean that there is no question to be answered; and this is not just in appreciation of the fact that outside the intellectual debate, with the press acting as a catalyzer for differing perspectives, issues of the 'truth-value' of representations remain central to the political debate and to political slander.[14]

Within the dominant theoretical discourse about realism in documentaries and documentary drama, any recourse to fact versus fiction comes over as entirely simplistic because the most basic assumption behind any discussion is the impossibility of naively appealing to 'the real' as an unconstructed, unmediated slice of life. Since unmediated reality does not exist on television, the analysis of forms of representation, of the relations between various discourses within the text, and the positioning of readers in relation to them, become central concerns. In postmodern theories it is the text and its relationship to other texts which replaces the analysis of the relationship between text and a given social reality, although there are differences among postmodernists as to how extreme they are in the denial of the existence of any non-textual referent. John Frow in an excellent article on intertextuality is aware of the danger of incorporating 'broad domains of social being . . . within the single conceptual domain of textuality' (Frow 1990: 54). With a social semiotic approach to discourse this risk does not arise since it foregrounds problems of interaction between social practices and the various conflicting discursive representations as they surface in the form of the semiotic levels of media texts and in the contestation of these representations by different readings and readers. Such an approach allows not only a full semiotic analysis of any number of texts as given semiotic constructs, but equally, in the same theoretical framework, the contestation and subversion of these through the clashing worlds of the referents and respondents.

The genre of social documentary through the medium of television allows little alternative but to represent through the symbolic, so the tension and the dynamic interchange between the specific and the general will remain endemic to any of its productions.

The makers of BB tried to cope with this inevitable dilemma by a clear upfronting of their own thesis. In this respect the series seems to me to be far less guilty of the charges that are levelled against it than *The Media Show* itself, which pretends to an analytical meta-perspective which is theoretically naive, to say the least. How far these or any other semiotic presentation of social issues can convince viewers to alter pre-existing beliefs and attitudes is, however, another issue altogether, and one that cannot be argued or predicted from within these presentations.

Conclusion

Breadline Britain gives a moving account of poverty existing in Britain today, and how widespread it is. In its representation of the poor, it is partial in stressing the sad and melancholic rather than other aspects of poverty where deprivation might provoke street fights, joy riding, and other forms of violent protest. It is not about anger and aggression, but about sadness, desolation and despair, about the 'deserving poor', who, as Boyce puts it in *The Media Show*, have somehow fallen through the social net. The programme thus does not provide any argument against the Tory MPs who declared joy-riding and street-fighting to be acts of the devil; who attacked the Archbishop of York for trying to find social causes for violence, and who prefer to see any such outbursts as pure evil. But its solid research basis, and its interweaving of the narratives of representative individuals with a clearly stated thesis make it an impressive documentation of poverty in the UK, which in my view cannot be assessed within the discourses of documentary film-making alone but has to be discussed as part of the politics and sociology of poverty.

Applying a socio-semiotic analysis to the particular question of how a television series approached the question of poverty involved an analysis of the transposition of social-scientific academic discourse into the semiotic codes of text, images, and music. In the interaction between these semiotic codes different styles of discourse were separating the narratives of individual 'poor people' from the general discussion of poverty in the UK today. Contestation of this presentation was offered from *The Media Show* which suggested a simplistic pre-modernist version of fact versus fiction. In the next chapter Kay Richardson will proceed with the different kinds of contestation and agreements offered by groups of actual viewers.

Notes

1. See, for example, television review programmes such as BBC2's *Did You See?* and the now discontinued Channel 4 series discussed here, *The Media Show*; or satirical programmes such as *Spitting Image* which depends to a large extent on intertextual references to other television programmes (Meinhof and Smith: in preparation).
2. For a quick review of the development of interest in the discourses of viewers see Richardson's chapter in this volume.
3. See also my footnote in Meinhof 1993: 222. 'With the terms "open" and "closed" I am borrowing the terminology of Eco (1981). My own usage differs from Eco's in that I am restricting the terms to different ways of interpreting texts. Eco, on the other hand, characterizes particular narratives as open or closed, depending on the range of interpretative proposals which the text validates.'
4. Income level is, of course, one of the more traditional, though not

uncontroversial ways of measuring poverty. See the bi-annual, not easily accessible publication of the DHSS, *Households Below Average Income*. In contrast see P. Townsend (1979) *Poverty in the United Kingdom. A Survey of Household Resources and Standards of Living* and J. Mack and S. Lansley's own 1985 publication, *Poor Britain*.

5. See for example *Daily Express*, 8 April 'Hard to Believe. There are lies, damned lies, and now, it seems London Weekend Television statistics' or the *Daily Mail*'s ironic comment on 26 April, 'A Very Poor Show [headline] ... The problem is to come up with a definition of poverty which produces such staggeringly large figures that they rekindle the sympathy of a society beginning to suffer from compassion fatigue.'

   Note that the *Daily Mail*'s comment taken out of its context could refer to the very real problem of representing the relative poverty in the UK at the sight of absolute poverty in Third World countries that Brian Street's article in this volume refers to. But the *Daily Mail*'s ironic jibe only serves as hostile denial of the existence of poverty in Britain altogether.

6. See *The Guardian* leader, 8/4/91 and *New Statesman*, 19/4/91.

7. For a collection of essays on documentary broadcasting see Corner (ed.) 1986.

8. Compare, for example, in *Did You See?*, the negative comments on documentaries of Remembrance Day with the praise of the concurrent repeat of *Testament of Youth*, a drama series about Vera Brittain's struggle through the First World War (October/November 1992).

9. Field/tenor/mode in Hallidayan linguistics are parameters of so-called 'situation types' which allow a systematic correlation to parts of the grammar. Field refers to social activity including subject matter, tenor to the interrelations among participants, mode to channel or medium. Each correlates with functional components of the semantic system which, in turn, correlate with typical realizations in grammar. For discussion of this see, for example, Halliday (1978).

10. See, for example, the argument about realism in Postmodernist critique, notably in the contributions of Christian Metz and Stephen Heath in *Screen*, and *Screen Reader 2*.

11. For a detailed exposition of displacement and dichotomy see Meinhof 1993: 216f.

12. I am grateful to Phillip Tagg from Liverpool University for his generous help with the analysis of the music.

13. As was already explained in the introduction, *The Media Show* is a Channel 4 series, broadcast before its recent discontinuation on prime time television on Sunday evenings. Moderated by Emma

Freud who succeeded Muriel Grey in that role, the series takes as its theme aspects of media policy and practices. Programmes typically draw on a range of practitioners or analysts from the field of media studies: journalists, producers, academics, and usually present a highly critical view of their subject matter.
14. See, for example, the row over advertisements by NALGO discussed by Street and Hewitt in Chapters 2 and 5.

References

Bakhtin, M. (1981) *The Dialogical Imagination*. Austin, Texas: University of Texas Press.

Corner, J. (1986) (ed.) *Documentary and the Mass Media*. London: Arnold.

DHSS (Department of Health and Social Security) *Households Below Average Income*. London: HMSO.

Eco, U. (1981) *The Role of the Reader*. London: Hutchinson.

Fish, S. (1980) *Is there a text in this class?* Cambridge, Mass: Harvard University Press.

Forster, E. M. (1910) *Howard's End*. London: Arnold.

Frow, J. (1990) 'Intertextuality and ontology'. In Warton, M. and Still, J. (eds) *Intertextuality: Theories and Practices*. Manchester: Manchester University Press.

Halliday, M. A. K. (1978) *Language as Social Semiotic*. London: Arnold.

Jakobson, R. (1960) 'Linguistics and Poetics'. In Sebeok, T. (ed.) *Style in Language*. Cambridge, Mass: MIT Press: 350–77.

Mack, J. and Lansley, S. (1985) *Poor Britain*. London: George Allen & Unwin.

Meinhof, U. H. and Smith, J. (eds.) (In preparation). *Intertextuality and the Media: from Genre to Everyday Life*.

Meinhof, U. H. (1993) 'Double-talk in news broadcasts.' In Graddol, D. and Boyd-Barrett, O. (eds.). *Media texts: Authors and Readers*. Clevedon: Multilingual Matters: 212–23.

Sandford, J. (1976) *Cathy Come Home*. London: Marion Boyars.

Screen Reader 2 (1981). *Cinema and Semiotics*. London: Society for Education in Film and Television.

Tagg, P. (1993) 'Universal' music and the case of death. In *Critical Quarterly*, 35: 2. 54–98.

Townsend, P. (1979) *Poverty in the United Kingdom. A Survey of Household Resources and Standards of Living*. London: Allen Lane.

Volosinov, V. N. (1973) *Marxism and the Philosophy of Language*. New York: Seminar Press.

Wilkinson, R. G. (1990) Income distribution and mortality: a 'natural' experiment. *Sociology of Health and Illness*, **12**: 391–412.

4 *Interpreting* Breadline Britain

Kay Richardson

The present chapter picks up where the previous one left off, in order to talk about the sense that viewers were able to make of *Breadline Britain*, especially programme 4 'No place like home'. It is one thing to present a textual analysis of a television programme or any other kind of mass media text. It is a different matter to say whether and how far the meanings which the *analyst* attributes to the programme are the 'realized meanings' so far as the viewers are concerned. It has become a commonplace in television audience research that viewers are not 'cultural dopes', and there would be no originality in a research project which simply sought to demonstrate once again that they are not. It is possible now to assume that viewers are not the victims of indoctrination by television, and to go beyond that point in seeking to show more exactly what kinds of meanings they construct from their viewing experiences, and the extent to which different kinds of viewers agree or disagree in their interpretations. To quite a large extent, the viewers that I talked to about 'No place like home' (programme 4 of *Breadline Britain*) agreed in their interpretation of it (though disagreeing in their responses to it, and to the individuals featured in it), in spite of the fact that their cultural positionings differed substantially.[1] Research which can demonstrate substantial viewer convergence in interpretation must be just as valuable as research which focuses upon divergence. Neither convergence nor divergence in itself necessarily entails that viewers have *passively* absorbed some textual or ideological meaning.

The complexity of these viewers' responses to the programme is what we have to consider, for it bears interestingly upon the key questions in television audience research:

1. How important are the images to the impact of the television message?
2. How do different representational strategies affect the way viewers make sense of programmes?
3. What difference does the viewer's cultural positioning make to his or her interpretation of the TV text?

Television audience research – the state of the art

Before I explain how exactly I went about the study, found viewers willing to watch 'No place like home', interviewed them, and analysed the taped discussions, it is necessary to contextualize the research in relation to current trends in television audience studies. A recent publication by Justin Lewis (1992) is a useful introduction to work in this field; for a more critical account, see Corner (1991).

Mass media texts are created in offices and studios, but they are received in a multiplicity of households, by people whose cultural positions vary widely. Along with the variations in cultural position go different value systems, differences of knowledge, and of cultural capital. It is reasonable to suppose that such variations make a difference when it comes to making sense of media output. In the audience research of the 1980s it became commonplace to read about the viewers' *active* sense-making practices. And textual analyses on their own, without reference to either the context of production or the context of reception, were increasingly marginalized as contributions to media scholarship.

In order to undertake research that would do justice to the interpretative variation that researchers now expected to find within the mass audience, the closed questionnaire associated with more positivist research traditions was abandoned in favour of extended and open-ended discussions with individual viewers or groups of viewers. In some studies viewers were selected not according to strict social-demographic characteristics like age, gender and so forth, but rather according to their social affiliations. In Corner et al. (1990) for example, a study that focuses upon reactions to programmes about the nuclear power industry and its risks, the groups chosen included activists in local branches of the political parties; members of environmentalist groups; workers within the industry; unemployed people; school-children and so forth. The assumption was that it would be such affiliations which could potentially provide viewers with distinctive meaning systems for making sense of the nuclear power issue. The new methods are sometimes described as 'ethnographic', because they are sensitive to these dimensions of social life. But in other recent work, the label 'ethnographic' is chosen also because researchers have interviewed people in the very homes where the viewing gets done. 'Families', it is argued, are the most important kind of social grouping upon which to concentrate. It should be appreciated that the methods favoured by media researchers stop well short of the long-term participant observation favoured in anthropology. There are drawbacks too in trying to establish a 'naturalistic' context for research: all comments that seem to be elicited from viewers in the 'artificial' setting of a research discussion or interview are regarded with excessive suspicion as data which is not to be wholly trusted as a source of evidence on the 'real' processes of viewing and understanding which take place in the home.

The point is well taken that people who do not normally talk at length and self-consciously about specific programmes are doing something slightly unnatural when they do so after a screening in a university seminar room or other 'public' space. However it does not follow from this that the kinds of things they *say* are unnatural in the sense that they do not represent the actual thoughts of speakers, from their various subject positions and drawing upon familiar, relevant discourses. Undoubtedly the comments made in these research settings are conditioned by the speech situation, which has its own interpersonal relations. But it would be hard to argue that the speech situation can be held responsible for the *substance* of the comments, except in the sense that they may have an interest in coming across as concerned citizens, and will want to say the things that they believe such citizens ought to say. For example, in the study I am about to report it was notable that the Townswomen's Guild were caught between their 'own' views and what they imagined they should believe.

The *Breadline Britain* viewers

For this study I screened one episode of the *Breadline Britain* series, programme 4 'No place like home', to selected groups of viewers and asked them for their reactions. I wanted to establish groups of viewers rather than screening the programme to single individuals. The point of this was that members of the group would be sufficiently familiar with one another to overcome any inhibitions they might feel. Also, the conversation after the screening (which was taped, with the knowledge of the viewers) could then take the form of a discussion between them, rather than an interview controlled entirely by me. Secondly, giving the research its quasi-ethnographic character (see discussion above) the groups themselves were selected on the basis of distinctive cultural positioning, and potentially very different ways of aligning themselves to the question of poverty in Britain. My hope of course was that those different alignments would produce different kinds of talk about the material screened.

I had no staff support for this research and only enough money to pay volunteers a small sum for their time, and to buy audiotapes. It was thus never intended to be more than a small-scale study whose findings might be suggestive. There are many more audience variables that could have been explored: different episodes of the series could have been shown to some groups; other programmes about poverty could have been considered. The limitations of the study in respect of its scale must be acknowledged. Nevertheless, it was worth undertaking. The participating groups varied in how close they themselves were to the experience of poverty. Of the six groups I will be concentrating upon, three are especially significant. These three are: the single parents, the Citizens Advice Bureau, the Townswomen's Guild.[2] The single parents were as close as I could get to viewers who shared the experiences depicted in the programme. The viewers from the Citizens Advice Bureau reacted to the people in the programme as they would to their own clients, and claimed 'professional' experience as the basis of their knowledge about the poor in Britain. And then there was the Townswomen's Guild. Their personal circumstances *in the present* put them at a considerable remove from personal or professional experience of poverty. For them, poverty today meant the tramps that they sometimes passed on the streets of Liverpool, and it meant representations of various kinds that had been mediated to them by the press, radio and television. This lack of familiarity with poverty in the present, however, was only part of the story. For, as it turned out (and I will have more to say about this below) they claimed a great deal of experience of poverty in the past, in their own childhood and early married years, and drew upon that experience extensively in the comments they made about 'No place like home'.

The other three groups in the study I can mention more briefly. A group referred to below as the 'Church group' consisted of only two people, the local Franciscan friar, and one other man who helped out at the friary in its charitable activities. The 'Youth group' consisted of a female youth leader and three males in their early twenties, all unemployed. And finally there was a second Townswomen's Guild group, from a different part of town from the first set.

All groups were invited to the University to watch 'No place like home', knowing only that the programme would be 'about poverty in Britain'. Each person was paid ten pounds for participating. All of the groups said yes when I asked them if they would like a copy of the transcription from the tape recording I made of the discussion. No-one who came found they had nothing at all to say, though, as you would expect, some individuals were very much more vocal than others. Many people offered their services again, should I need their help with a future project.

After the recordings had been duly transcribed, the process of analysis began, and the results are presented below. This did not involve the exhaustive coding of each transcript according to a strict set of criteria. But there were particular themes I wanted to focus upon, themes which emerged from the discussion itself, not ones I had anticipated, or structured into the interview pro forma. For example there was the 'political' theme – the extent to which viewers detected a political slant to the programme (mostly they saw no political slant). In the end I was not able to follow through the political theme, but one that I did follow through was the one on the importance of visual images for viewers' interpretations. This theme became very important in the analysis, and is discussed fully below (Image as evidence: can you believe what you see?).

In what follows I have used quotations selectively, to illustrate particular points that I wanted to make about the data. The analysis itself was more systematic: it involved going through each transcript with reference to about eight distinct themes, not all of which were developed for the purposes of this chapter. We can now turn our attention to the results of the analysis.

Us and them: the relevance of personal experience

As already mentioned, the groups which participated in this study were selected on the basis of their variable relations to the experience of poverty, with the Townswomen's Guild at one end of the spectrum, and the single-parent families at the other end. It was to be expected that these differences among the viewers would affect their interpretations of, and reactions to the programme. As previous research suggests, one of the things that viewers commonly do, is relate their own experiences and knowledge to what they are seeing and hearing from the television (see Dahlgren 1988; Hoijer 1990; Jensen 1986; Seiter et al. 1989). They compare televised subjects (i.e. individuals mediated by TV) with themselves, their own backgrounds and present circumstances, or with other people known to them through face-to-face social networks. The extent and type of such comparison varies, of course, depending upon the nature of the programme. Discussions of the exchange rate mechanism provide much less scope for it than material about unemployment, education, football hooliganism, and so on – 'social issues', broadly defined. Then, the representational strategy that a programme employs can be more or less congenial to the desire to compare. 'No place like home', with its film reports taking individual households to represent social groupings, is more congenial in that sense than a studio discussion between interested parties.

There are viewer variables too. Viewers differ in the nature of the experience that they can draw upon, and that they thematize as relevant to the context of the discussion, as the following quotations show:

1. TOWNSWOMEN'S GUILD 1
    As Renie said, we were in poverty when we were little. But I don't know, maybe it was a different kind of poverty. At least we were clean and fed. A lot of these people, they just don't

seem to care at all in my opinion. They won't help themselves, a lot of them. The councils do have a lot to account for. They don't . . . as far as housing is concerned, some of those places are really terrible. But there again, when we were young, our parents kept . . . I mean, those walls, paper coming off the walls, the paint and things like that . . . although we didn't have any money our parents kept their houses clean and in repair. They didn't rely on their landlords to do those things, they did it for themselves, for their own comfort and for our comfort.

2. SINGLE PARENTS

Like I said, I've been homeless, I've been on the street when I was a bare sixteen, so I know what they mean, and how they feel, and what they're saying, you know, it's a really horrible feeling, horrible way to be, way to live.

3. CHURCH

I know loads of people in London who beg, I know loads of them, and they're all pulling eighty-ninety quid a day. I'm not joking. That's not poor, they can go and book in a hotel. I know one or two who do book in a hotel. But not everybody's like that, I mean the ones who sit there and beg, I don't understand why they should, because there's food, they want food [sic]. And I don't mind people begging for housing, if they're going to beg up their money for a flat, [its a way of getting] a couple of hundred pounds. So if you begged up your money for a flat, got your flat, made your claim and then started from there. But for some reason they don't, they get lost.

4. CITIZENS ADVICE BUREAU

But I remember on him, [individual with defective gas cooker from programme 1 of *Breadline Britain*] when I was discussing him with Manweb, and he said 'I don't believe that programme, that was exaggerated'. And I said 'excuse me'. And I reeled off a big list of clients that I'd dealt with, with him, so it wasn't a breach of confidentiality. I said, 'all those people are worse off than anybody in that programme, if you want to talk about relative poverty'.

For the Townswomen's Guild it is relevant and appropriate to talk about their own personal experiences of poverty, back in the 1930s. The single parent who draws upon her memory of homelessness at 17 is a woman in her early forties: poverty in the 1960s has a different kind of resonance from that of the Depression years. In the Church group it is a youth in his early twenties who claims to know homeless people in the present (elsewhere he draws upon his own recent experience of homelessness too). The speaker in extract 4, also in her early forties, recounts a conversation she had had about this very series when it was originally screened. In that conversation she had been able to counter a sceptical reading of the programme by reference to shared knowledge of people familiar to her and her interlocutor in their professional roles – she as a Citizens Advice Bureau worker and activist in a Right to Fuel action group, and he as her contact within the electricity company.

Interesting too in this selection of quotations are the variations of rhetorical strategy. To start with 2 (single parents) – here the point is to use personal experience not only to endorse the truth of the representation, but in accepting that truth, to claim empathy with the subject on the basis of the latter's own discourse within the programme. *To know is to know the same, and to know the same is to feel the same.* By contrast, in 3 (church) personal experience functions to deny an automatic connection between begging and poverty: by implication this move *challenges* the truth of the representation, which has taken that connection on trust throughout. *To know is to know different.* Personal experience in 1 (Townswomen's Guild) is not used to challenge the truthfulness of the programme; rather, the point here is to resist the claim to sympathy made by and on behalf of the subjects. These viewers know that they are being invited to feel sorry for Yvonne, Jackie and Kim. They refuse the invitation. They want more than proof of poverty before their sympathy will be bestowed – they want virtue, too, and they won't take that on trust, but require the evidence. And this is because they remember when poverty and virtue did go together, when the deprivation was even worse. *To know (remember) is to feel differently.* Number 4 (Citizens Advice Bureau) is like 2 in that personal experience for this viewer accords with what the programme says about Yvonne, Jackie and Kim (and thus about the social groups that these three subjects stand for). It is made more interesting than 2 by virtue of the fact that it occurs in the context of a (reported) *debate* about truthfulness. Any gap between truth and reality for this speaker would be a gap the converse of the one her interlocutor wants to claim: 'All those people are worse off than anybody in that programme.' But she seems to stop short of challenging the programme in this respect. The existence of people who are worse off than *Breadline Britain*'s subjects does not make *Breadline Britain* false for her. *To know is to know more.*

There is a final point to be made in this section, under the rubric of *reflexivity*. The group which is the most reflexively aware of how their own experiences are informing their judgements, is the Townswomen's Guild. To some extent this is apparent even from the very short extract reproduced as quotation 2 above. It is more apparent when the entire transcript is taken into account. It was even reflected in the talk that I exchanged with these women after the screening and discussion session was over, and the audiotape recorder switched off. At this point it took the form of group members saying to me that they hoped I had 'got what I wanted' from the session, and expressing their anxiety that they were the 'wrong people' to talk to about this particular programme. The basis for this anxiety, I think, was their sense that they had not responded to the subjects sympathetically, even though the programme had intended them to do so. And somehow my intentions in talking to them, and the programme's intentions, had become conflated. They took my point that their unsympathetic reaction was just as interesting as a more generous one, but there was nevertheless at various points in the discussion a lurking sense that their *generation* disqualified them from judging the programme. (It did not stop them doing so, though – they just hedged their judgements in those terms.) In a sense they are right. The programme speaks the liberal discourse of poverty. It is interested in relative deprivation within the country at a given time (the 1990s), and also in historical shifts, so that the point of the programme is whether or not the poor have shared in the increasing affluence of the society as a whole (they seem not to have done so). This liberal discourse is not the discourse of the Townswomen. Theirs is the conservative discourse, of self-help, self-improvement, the virtue of saving, the vice of extravagance, the shame of poverty and the importance of concealing it:

5.   TOWNSWOMEN'S GUILD 2
     It was nothing to see children barefoot.
     Oh no.
     And they were all happy. You never thought . . . And they never went round telling everybody because their mother or their

father would just clip them when they went in, and said 'I hope
you haven't told that neighbour we're that hard up'. The pride
was terrific, going back all those years. There's no pride today,
there's no manners today.

They understand well enough that the value system they are
remembering is not one that is now normatively enforced. In
engaging with the programme they are engaging with the great
cultural shifts that have taken place since the inter-war years, in
relation to their own histories as girls, then wives and mothers,
then grandmothers (they also talked about the younger genera-
tions of their own families during the discussions). In hearing the
encounter of the Townswomen's Guild with *Breadline Britain* as
an encounter between conservative and liberal discourses, it is
instructive to note that the less conservatively minded groups
reproduced exactly the same encounter, in part by *mimicking* the
still-potent conservative discourse with which they are all too
familiar, though they reject it. They cannot produce this encounter
by engaging with the programme, which to varying degrees they
approve of, only by engaging with *other viewers* of the
programme, not present at the discussion and so imagined into
being, as thus:

6. SINGLE PARENTS
    'Don't you think?', 'Shouldn't have got pregnant', 'You
    shouldn't have left home to be on the street', 'You shouldn't
    have got pregnant, you shouldn't have been homeless, you
    should get out and go to work and stop being a parasite'. That's
    their attitude, people who've got money, they're the worst.
    'You're just a load of scum, drop dead'.

That the imaginary projection draws upon concrete experiences
is evidenced by another contribution from a member of this
group, of an extremely relevant kind:

7. SINGLE PARENTS
    All our sympathy doesn't count for anything, because we related
    to them. I'll give you an example. I was in the pub on Monday
    night, taxi drivers' pub, and they were talking about that
    programme on ITV, *World in Action*, and the taxi driver sitting
    next to us, he said, 'What do you think of all these people
    begging on the streets and all that?' And he said 'They're scum.'
    'Parasites', he said, 'I'd lock them all up.'

The reference here is to the *World in Action* series which had a middle-class lawyer live the life of a destitute person, on the streets, trying to eat, sleep, find accommodation, claim benefits and so on, all with a concealed camera in his bag.

Neither of these contributions refer to *Breadline Britain* in particular. Number 6 is non-specific, and 7 relates to *World in Action*. The discussion also included attempts to work through these ideas in relation to Kim, Jackie and Yvonne. A viewer in one group approves the choice of Kim as a subject because, he thinks, she can be seen as an innocent victim:

8.   CHURCH GROUP
    Can I just go back a bit to the young homeless? I think it made good points about that because I think there's a lot of popular thought about young homeless people being there because they want to be there, and they've chosen that, and I think it addresses some of the issues about that in terms of . . . I mean, the girl portrayed is from a children's home, and from working in special education, there's a lot of problems round that, so I thought it was good that that was shown.

That the programme makers picked Kim as a relatively deserving case is a plausible supposition, especially as her children's home background is specifically mentioned in the programme. Other sympathetic viewers are less certain than this speaker that Kim's background will in itself be enough to silence the conservative voice:

9.   SINGLE PARENTS
    Although people would say that girl, obviously she must have run away from a council children's home or something, they said she was seventeen and been on the streets for two years. Now she knows that she can go back into a home but she won't because she doesn't like it, but people will say, 'Well, that's her decision.'

Showing, telling and claiming: the limits of credibility

In this section and the next I want to focus less upon the viewer variables and more upon the programme itself. The present section follows on from the foregoing discussion in that it is concerned broadly with *Breadline Britain*'s credibility for viewers. But the focus above was principally upon the ways that personal and professional experience allows viewers to challenge either the truthfulness of the programme or to resist the emotional reaction that it is perceived as attempting to elicit. By contrast, here I am concerned to show that challenge and resistance is not just a matter of knowing things about society that *Breadline Britain* does not know – it is a matter, too, of according different kinds of credibility to different aspects of the programme's formal and rhetorical organization.

It is useful to distinguish between the *shown* (i.e. the images and their referents), the *told* (less image-able propositional information) and the *claimed* (propositions whose credibility depends upon the presentation of appropriate argument and evidence). In many programmes of course, and *Breadline Britain* is no exception, it is in terms of *implied* meanings that 'claiming' gets done. The credibility of the programme depends upon the interaction of all three of these levels of representation. The level of the shown, I want to deal with separately: the purpose of the present section is to explore the tension between telling and claiming, with especial reference to the programme's strategy of using 'representative' case histories.

There is one aspect of the tension between telling and claiming that arises directly from the use of case histories: the familiar problem of *typicality* (or, more loosely, *representativeness*). The fault-line of credulousness is the line that says: 'I believe what they say about X. But I don't believe that X is typical of the category.' And if X is not typical, then there is a licence to believe things about the category that are not true of X. In the case of *Breadline Britain*, then, from the fact that Kim, Jackie and Yvonne are deserving cases, nothing follows (though for the Townswomen's Guild the three of them are *not* unequivocally deserving cases). And it is not even necessary to refer to the case histories on the programme, as extract 10 shows:

10.   TOWNSWOMEN'S GUILD 2
      I think some of them bring it on themselves. They don't particularly want to work. And some of them that have money, they spend it on the wrong things. When they do get their allowances, they don't always spend it economically really.

'They' here does not refer to Kim, Jackie and Yvonne, but to poor people in general. For *Breadline Britain* to establish by evidence and argument the typicality of these cases would have been a difficult task. No 'real' case can ever instantiate all and only the most common features of any given category – whatever that might mean. There are too many variables to take into account, and idiosyncrasy can never be eliminated. The series does have a more quantitative account of the poor in Britain, but that is in a different programme from the one I used for this study. I am only concerned to point out that the case study strategy in a sense invites this kind of response. The viewers who participated in the research understood the strategy well enough – that more was at stake than the lives of Kim, Jackie and Yvonne, rhetorically speaking. The viewers, in all groups, repeatedly addressed themselves to the larger stakes, overriding in their reception of the programme its implication that these specific cases are good, representative examples of the general situation of the poor in Britain.

This does not necessarily mean that they had nothing to say about the lives of Kim, Jackie and Yvonne, though I did sometimes have to prompt them into talking about the case histories. I wanted to hear them relate the case histories to their ideas about the poor in general, divided up for the purpose of this episode into people with different types of unacceptably low housing conditions. Two specific patterns emerged. Pattern number one was articulated as 'We don't have enough information'. Pattern number two came out as 'There are much worse cases than these'. There were other variations too, (e.g. 'People who beg aren't necessarily poor' – see extract 2 above) but these two were the ones that recurred.

'We don't have enough information'

The Townswomen's Guild groups never said in so many words that the case histories were untypical and the programme therefore dishonest. They had their own beliefs about the poor, as discussed in the previous section, but tended to produce these as alternative accounts of poverty to the one provided in the programme, rather than using their beliefs to challenge the programme in a direct way. Engaging with the case studies gave them some difficulty, because, if they were accepted as true in themselves, they could not easily be used as a resource for the belief that the poor 'bring it on themselves'. Hence the awkwardness in the following extract, and the resort to speculation about the degree of artifice that has gone into producing the stories:

11.   TOWNSWOMEN'S GUILD
When we were all brought up, we were all . . . you just got a jolly good hiding, told to be quiet and go upstairs. And that was the end of it. But today they walk out, and I think that's
. . .
(*KR*: Do you think that was the case with the woman, the girl that they actually used in this programme to represent the situation of the homeless?)
She was on quite a lot wasn't she?
(*KR*: Yes)
She was a tough sort of person I'd say.
She was.
But they all knew they were being photographed. They agreed to it. And did they get paid?

Because they do find assessing the cases hard, for one of the two Townswomen's Guild groups it becomes an issue of *information* (and the lack of it) in the programme. They cannot judge how deserving these cases are, because they do not know enough about the circumstances. The poverty itself is not sufficient: they need to know how the three women came to be in the situations they are in:

12.   TOWNSWOMEN'S GUILD
We don't really know much about her other than what we saw on there. It makes a vast difference if she could get that little child into a nursery, and could get a job. It didn't go into that did it. She didn't say 'I tried to get a job and can't.' She was grumbling about what she hadn't got.

But it is not only the Townswomen who complain about lack of information. The Citizens Advice Bureau group made the same complaint:

13.   CITIZENS ADVICE BUREAU

It didn't show why she was living, how she got to live in that
house [Yvonne]. And people think, who don't understand any
better, that you've got options. She was obviously to my view
trying to do her best in an extremely difficult situation. She was
the only one who actually verbalized the stigma attached to
poverty and how she would like to be able to invite people
back to a clean house, and I'd be saying to myself 'well, why is
she carrying that pram up the stairs, why isn't she on the
ground floor?' and so on. But we're working in a particular
sphere where we will, we'll look out for things like that, and
question things like that. And I think people who have not got
personal or professional experience, well we want them to
know why they're in that situation. Is it their own fault?

There is of course an important difference between the terms of
this speaker's complaint and those of the speaker in extract 12.
The speaker in 12 is objecting on her own behalf – she wants to
make moral judgements and she cannot. The speaker in 13 has
made her judgement: 'She was obviously to my view trying to do
her best in an extremely difficult situation.' But she is also
concerned with the potential effect of this representation upon
other people with less experience and knowledge than herself, and
with different preconceived ideas. Once again this can be seen as
two differently contextualized manifestations of the encounter
between the liberal and the conservative discourse on poverty,
where the liberally minded viewers have to produce the conservative discourse as the voice of 'others', by mimicking it as in extract
6, while the conservatively minded have made that discourse their
own. Yet in 13 we do have a much milder version of the
conservative discourse in play – the other viewers envisaged here
are not the rabidly prejudiced ones of extract 6, but a more
puzzled and perhaps open minded set who might take the view,
with a bit more background information to help them, that
Yvonne is there through no fault of her own.

'There are much worse cases than these'

It is of interest that one of the Townswomen's Guild members
took a line that: 'They never focus on the people who are really
poor', glossing the really poor as: 'older people who have had big

families and have never had good husbands and never been able to save anything'. Other, more sympathetic, groups also tended to feel that *Breadline Britain* had not picked the worst cases of poverty in Britain, though without specifying in as much detail as this what the 'worst cases' were like. The single parents all agreed with the speaker who said:

14. SINGLE PARENTS
    I thought it was very good, well represented, but I would say there's a lot of people are living in much worse conditions than them people showed on that programme, much worse. I'd say they're not the bottom line of it all.

I do not take this to be a straightforward criticism of the programme for failing to pick the most extreme cases. That would suggest the speaker perceived the programme's strategy to be based on a principle of extremeness rather than a principle of typicality (a different way of connecting the specific with the general). There is evidence that she does not perceive the strategy in these terms; she goes along with what the next speaker has to say on this point:

15. SINGLE PARENTS
    I thought the programme was very good. I think really what it does show is the in-between of the poverty line, there are some people who are worse off, there are people who are better off, that is like in the middle, it's more realistic. It goes over better. If you go too far down people tend not to . . . They brush it under the carpet, 'cos they think, 'Oh well, they're there because they're there.' But that, really, those people, to my mind were there through no fault of their own, and that came over.

Nevertheless, the existence of worse cases is for the first speaker and for the group as a whole an important proviso to their acceptance of the programme's version of reality, just as the existence of beggars 'pulling eighty-ninety quid a day' is an important proviso for the youth in the church group (extract 2). For all of the groups, there was a point at which they became exercised by the problem of realism versus sympathy, as a representational dilemma for programmes of this sort. That is to say, they recognize that the programme is trying to elicit sympathy; they also recognize that it is trying to be faithful to reality. Visions of *extreme* distress and disadvantage would help towards the former objective, yet would involve a sacrifice of realism, since not all of the poor are living at the extreme edge of poverty. This dilemma was particularly appreciated in relation to the absence of confrontation in the lives of the subjects, something that was noted by all of the groups but most articulately in one:

16.   YOUTH GROUP
I felt particularly where they went to the housing office that the people would have asked them to reserve ... in advance to reserve their reactions to what the people were saying because when [they're] in that situation, people, although it doesn't do them good all the time they tend to get aggressive in that situation, because of the frustration that they're feeling. And if you've been going along to the housing office for so many weeks, I don't think I'd be able to sit there and say 'OK then how long's it going to be, OK then, thanks very much.'
(*KR*: You think she was too polite?)
I think she'd probably been directed in that direction, for the sake of the programme. But you could argue that that sheds positive light upon the people in poverty because they get through their position with dignity. It's the thing of not knowing whether it's real or not, because of the way it's been presented. A lot of truth can be hidden.

The above extract shows how speculations about the reality status of elements in the featured case histories can come to be on the agenda as the result of an externalized train of thought that begins with the question of typicality/representativeness: 'is it usually like this?' turns into 'is *this* like this, really?' It is this area that I want to consider next, for it brings in the question of the visual images and the power that they exercise over viewer interpretations.

Image as evidence: can you believe what you see?

On the basis of the present study, the answer to the question 'Can you believe what you see?' would seem to be – yes, you can. That is to say, there is a strong predispositon where visual images are concerned to treat the television screen as 'a window on the world', though this predisposition is vulnerable when it comes to talking through reactions to a programme, as in the present study. And the visual images do need verbal support: the screen alone cannot establish what the images are images of. General scepticism about the manipulative practices of television (a scepticism which was quite widespread in the groups I talked to) does not, somehow, get 'cashed' in terms of systematic disbelief or agnosticism at the level of referentiality.

To say that viewers trust the veracity of images is a strong claim, and the principal evidence for it is negative. The question of referential truth, generally speaking, does not come up in the discussions until I introduce it by explaining the controversy over the 'sleeping rough' scene. This controversy is discussed by Ulrike Meinhof in the previous chapter. I made a point of telling every group that I talked to about it, and asking them for their reactions. Until that point, most groups simply talked 'as if' Kim, Yvonne and Jackie were real people, 'as if' the bodies on the screen were the bodies of those real people, 'as if' their encounters with bureaucrats were live events, 'as if' their material circumstances were as the programme depicted them, both verbally and visually.

17.   SINGLE PARENTS
In some ways the girl that was in the bed and breakfast is worse off though, than the girl who had the flat, because the girl who had the flat, although she had the bad conditions around the flat she had a bit more room to manoeuvre round, although she had a lot of small children.
And it was her own.
Yes. But the girl Jackie in that bed and breakfast, she was just confined, totally, to that one room.

Word and image-derived meanings have been woven into a fabric of belief about Yvonne and Jackie here, but there would seem to be no doubt in the speaker's mind that there are such people and he has seen pictures of them and heard and seen how they live. There is an exception to this pattern – one of the Citizens Advice Bureau group asks me if the people on screen are actors. He goes on to explain why he thought they might be:

18.   CITIZENS ADVICE BUREAU
Well, that girl that's homeless struck me as very casual. She's
sitting there saying, 'Spare a copper'. If you're passing, and a
bit interested. The next thing she's sitting there smoking and
chatting away. 'Where did you sleep last night.' I half expected
her to say, 'the Ritz' or something like that, rather than say,
'Oh God, I never got a wink of sleep all night.'

There is a problem about these 'performed' self-representations,
which are perhaps somewhat less convincing than if they *had*
employed actors. The speaker here is not the only one to think so,
but he is the only one to speculate that the programme has made
use of actors. Elsewhere it takes more cautious form – for
example, many groups were inclined to say when asked about
contrivance that certain scenes must have been affected by the
presence of the camera:

19.   YOUTH GROUP
I don't think it can be totally real because all the time there's a
camera there. And there's people with lights, and whatever, so
straightaway it's an act. It's not an act, but . . .
. . . it's controlled.

It is one thing to produce an argument saying that a scene must
be modified away from the real because it is television, and a
different thing to say that the performance was perceived as a
modified reality during the screening. The former is a deduction
which makes no reference to the text; the latter is a perception of
the text. The former can be used to explain the latter, or it can (as
here) occur on its own. Having considered the former as a
theoretical possibility, one can ask oneself *retrospectively* if the
performance confirms the possibility. Most commonly, this is
what the viewers I spoke to seem to have done.

Only one speaker in all of the groups appreciates that what's
going on is more than just a certain 'playing up' to the cameras in
an otherwise 'real' scene – note that it is in response to a question
by me about contrivance:

20.   SINGLE PARENTS
(*KR*: Do you think there were any scenes that were contrived
especially for the cameras?)
I thought that one in the housing office might have been

because they had a camera inside and a camera outside so both
places, both points of view, you know.

Because viewers do basically trust in the referentiality of visual
images, they can make use of what they see on the screen in
presenting their interpretations of the programme. Sometimes they
articulate visual meanings that have been reinforced by verbal
commentary. It is not surprising that most of the groups have
something to say about the terrible condensation and damp in
Yvonne's council flat, for that has been strongly foregrounded. As
Ulrike Meinhof has shown in the previous chapter, this is a
programme which, uncharacteristically in factual television, has a
verbal track which frequently refers to the concurrent visual
images in directly referential terms:

21.   CITIZENS ADVICE BUREAU
      Because the girl in the flat who had all the water coming down,
      that was obviously bad insulation, bad housing, it's not ...
      You can get condensation in the bathroom but you don't get it
      in your bedroom as a norm because that's normally where you
      do keep the baby warm, in the bedroom.

In other cases it is circumstantial details of the screen image which
are picked up and used as a resource in developing an
interpretation: details which are not reinforced on the verbal track
and which are probably not meant by the programme-makers to
be taken as intentionally/strategically presented. In the most
notable instance of this, concerning the jewellery worn by Jackie
and her son, the meaning which the Townswomen's Guild
attribute to that jewellery is as evidence of Jackie's extravagance.
Such an interpretation only makes sense as a 'transparent' reading
of something that they can see for themselves, *in spite of* the
programme-makers' sympathetic intentions:

22.   TOWNSWOMEN'S GUILD 2
      The girl in the bedsit, she's got two lots of ear-rings I think and
      quite a number of chains. If I was desperate for money, if I was
      in that position, I'd sell them, if they were worth anything,

which I think today a lot of them are. Because I've seen youngsters myself out of work and they've got better jewellery than I'll ever have. And I say to myself 'where on earth do they get them if they're not working?' Unless their parents or their families buy them, I don't know. But that's the first thing I thought. If they've got lots of jewellery on and it's worth anything I would certainly sell it if I had a little child and I didn't have much money.

Both of the Townswomen's Guild groups mention the jewellery in these terms, but none of the other groups refer to it at all.

Which brings me to the 'sleeping rough' scene, and the effect upon viewers of revealing to them that two of the lads in that scene had hostel accommodation, and had asked to be in the film. Viewers vary in how troubled they are by the revelation. There is no particular pattern to this variation according to the viewers' degree of sympathy with the programme's intentions, their alignments with conservative versus liberal discourses of poverty, their generational differences, group affiliations, or any other variable that I was able to consider. We can compare the reasoning used in one case where the viewers object and in one where they see no problem:

23.   CITIZENS ADVICE BUREAU
      If the research isn't done properly and you've got a situation like that and it becomes public that in actual fact they were in a hostel, that puts the doubt in other people's minds of whether the other isn't genuine then. That man was only pretending to be coming down the stairs, disabled, that house, that woman doesn't live in it, what's her name, Kim, Yvonne?

The speaker is right of course from a logical point of view, and many others made the same point. But note that it is still the effect on *other people* which is her primary concern. Its effect on *her* does not accord with her own scenario. Notwithstanding what she has just learned, *she* does not now think that the disabled man could have been pretending. She and the rest of the group continue to think that he was the genuine article. There are no cases in my tapes where a viewer reacts by collapsing into the generalized scepticism about referentiality that this speaker and

many others declared, with varying degrees of confidence, should
be the result of learning about this 'trickery'.

Other groups see no problem with the creation of the screen
image by these means:

> 24. TOWNSWOMEN'S GUILD
>   (*KR*: How do you feel about that, do you think you've been
>   conned?)
>   Well, don't you think that might be an isolated case really? Do
>   you mean that somebody would want to muscle in on the
>   programme? I don't think it would be done a lot really.
>   No I don't think so. No, I mean, they had slept rough,
>   probably, hadn't they, before?
>   (*KR*: Oh yes)
>   You can understand that.

Now this group see the *potential* problem in terms of
individuals deceiving the programme-makers and thus the viewers,
rather than being at all concerned with the idea that this is a
deception perpetrated by the programme-makers. But the terms of
their defence would apply if they'd taken the latter approach: it's
not dishonest because it's probably a one-off and anyway, if
they'd slept rough before they're not exactly fake examples of the
category they're being used to represent. It is not necessary to refer
to effects upon other viewers to develop this position. Even when
they're asked if it's a dishonest thing for the *programme-makers* to
do they see no reason to object:

> 25. TOWNSWOMEN'S GUILD 2
>   I don't think that was [dishonest]. I think if the whole scene
>   was manipulated, with everybody groaning and crying, well I
>   would think that was . . .

So *The Media Show* need not have worried. On finding out about
the substitution of 'fake' homeless people for 'real' ones, there are
two possible reactions. In one case people object, while simultaneously showing that their objection does not hold, i.e. it does
not hold *for them*. They are exceptions to their own rule that this
practice deceives. All of the objectors in the survey reacted in this
way, and I think it is reasonable to assume that this kind of

discrepancy between one's own viewing and that of other viewers is not something peculiar to the groups that I interviewed (see Richardson and Corner 1986 for similar evidence). And in the other case, more straightforwardly, they see no problem. The irony of all this is that from the point of view of media literacy and media critique among ordinary viewers, one might want to say that it is undesirable for viewers to trust the pictures as much as they seem to do.

Comparisons: degrees of scepticism and sympathy

Is it now possible to make any generalizations about the differences between the various groups, to support or undermine the hypothesis that cultural positioning gives rise to distinctive meaning systems which produce different interpretations of media texts?[3] I began this chapter by arguing that the viewing groups converged quite broadly in their interpretation of the programme, though diverging in their responses to it and in their degree of sympathy for the individuals. To reinforce this point, let me compare a couple of extracts where divergence of response overlays convergence of interpretation. A sympathetic group and an unsympathetic one concur in challenging the programme's realism on the same point: each group thinks that a greater degree of hostility, aggression, resentment, anger (the terms vary) is to be expected from people in poor circumstances, for example, in conversations with representatives of the bureaucracies that they have to deal with, in benefit offices, and so on. We can treat this as a matter of interpretation in that the perception of the encounters as rather polite is a shared perception. The only divergence between them is that in one case the fellow feeling is extended towards the institutional representative, and in the other, towards the supplicant, in ways that you might expect given the differences of cultural positioning:

26.   TOWNSWOMEN'S GUILD 2
      And it didn't show the fact that they often attack the people
      that are trying to help them, don't they. I mean they were very
      nice with each other but I don't think they all would be.
      No, I wouldn't think so.
      Wth the social services they wouldn't.

They even have cages round them, don't they?
They have terrible arguments. I feel sorry for the people round the counter.
It's terrible, it really is. It's not fair to them. They're only working, they're only doing a job.

27.   YOUTH GROUP
(*KR*: Was it just the politeness of it that made you feel, 'Oh, this can't be real, this must be done for the cameras', because it was too polite? Was that the giveaway?)
Well I'd say yes. There would have been a lot more swearing going on, and things like that.
(*KR*: Supposing they had shown that, supposing they'd done it that way?)
I think it would have put their backs up, [show] people in poverty in a worse light probably, for people looking at it. But that's the reality.
At the same time that is the reality and that's how down people can get, in that situation, like Alec was saying, they can't control their aggressiveness even though it's not a good thing to let it out in certain ways, like threatening the girl. Sometimes people who live in that position, they're more or less forced into that reaction, mentally they can't cope with it and they're going there all the time.

Most of the differences between the groups are differences of response rather than of interpretation, and it is at this level that I differentiate between the sympathetic groups (the Church group, the Youth group, the Citizens Advice Bureau and the single parents) and the unsympathetic ones (both Townswomen's groups). There are some differences of interpretation, but I will mention only one to avoid giving the impression that there was a lot of divergence. The one I will mention is not a trivial one, even though it seems to involve only one speaker in one group diverging from all the rest in every group. All of the groups but one *disagreed* with the idea that the programme had a political slant, or a bias of its own: they took the view that it was just 'stating facts' (some thought this lack of an angle was a fault – they wanted more discussion of the politics behind poverty, like the policy of the right to buy council houses, and the impact of that policy). In one group only is there an attempt to argue that the programme has a political position, and the speaker who suggests this comes up against resistance from other members of the group. The extract is so interesting that it is worth reproducing at length, with a couple of short edits. I have also tried to differentiate the various speakers who contribute to the discussion:

28. TOWNSWOMEN'S GUILD 1

A: What they're wanting us to know is the poverty in the country isn't it, that things are terrible. To me, they're making out how bad it is, and perhaps anti-government in a way, anti-Conservative government.

[Some non-relevant comments edited out.]

A: But I think a lot of them are geared against and are anti-government.

(*KR*: Was that programme anti-government?)

A: Well I suppose in a way it must be mustn't it? You know, people are living like this, and the government ... We are responsible for everything which automatically comes down to the government nowadays. And they're biased, a lot of it is biased towards socialism and socialism is the answer to everything.

[Some non-relevant comments edited out.]

B: There was only one girl who commented though, about her social security not being enough.

A: Again that comes down to the government doesn't it, the government is responsible. It could be anti-government in a way. Don't you think so?

B: I don't know, that's not how it came across [?] I don't know who they were blaming.

A: I always think a lot of these programmes are to me anti-government. I don't know if I'm right or not.

(*KR*: If that was anti-government I suppose it would be by implication rather than explicit?)

A: Not explicit, this is again, manipulation, can be manipulation can't it, like propaganda in a way, propaganda is manipulation.

[Some non-relevant comments edited out.]

B: No I wouldn't think so [that the programme is too biased for broadcasting during an election campaign]. I think it could have the opposite impact. I would think that they would think well any government that comes into power has got to be faced with this problem. That was my opinion of it.

A: Do you think so, oh.

B: Because no government's going to solve that problem.
A: I think it could turn people against the government that's in power, could influence them in some ways to say the others might be better, do something for these people.
B: Well yes, maybe.

It is fascinating to see this speaker sticking to her line that the programme is anti-government, arguing to an extent that such programmes always are, rather than being able to point to anything in the text itself, but also working out an underlying logic whereby it is valid to draw the inference that the government, being a Conservative government and not just any government, is to blame for poverty.

If differences at the level of interpretation are minimal, differences of response are real enough, as this chapter has, I hope, shown. Though I want to conclude this section by suggesting that even my distinction between the 'sympathetic' and the 'unsympathetic' groups is too simplistic and does not do justice to the complexity of the material.

Take the 'unsympathetic' Townswomen. They come across as unsympathetic because they declare themselves to be so, early on in the discussion. Then, in their comments about the poor in Britain, they show their lack of sympathy, and their desire to be convinced that the poor in 'No place like home' were deserving cases. But later they undermined their initial rejection of the programme's appeal to their sympathy in talking about the individual cases presented in the programme:

29.   TOWNSWOMEN'S GUILD 1
(*KR*: You didn't react sympathetically then to the girl who was homeless?)
[Confusion about who I am referring to, corrected within the group.]
(*KR*: I was meaning the girl who was homeless, living on the streets.)
Living on the streets.
I felt sympathetic to her . . .
In a way, yes
. . . because she'd been in care all her life, and then they throw them out on the streets, don't they. They're just thrown out and they have no proper home.

The Townswomen's Guild are equivocal, certainly – compare this extract with 22 above, where they suggest that Jackie might not be doing enough to help herself. And they themselves become uneasy in talking sympathetically about Kim, Jackie or Yvonne, after having tried to present an unsympathetic face at the general level.

Extract 29 brings me to the final arguments of this chapter. Taken together, the transcripts suggest that experience of contemporary poverty alone is neither a necessary nor sufficient condition for producing a 'deconstructive' reading of this text in which the meanings produced are attributed to the programme-makers rather than the subjects. The speaker in extract 29 has no such experience, and yet it is she more than anyone else I spoke to who gets furthest in trying to connect a generalized scepticism about 'the media's' intentions and practices with an analysis of this particular programme. I attribute this once again to the fact that she is speaking from a subject position inside the conservative discourse on poverty, has recognized a mismatch between that position and the discourse deployed by the programme, and is trying to get a 'handle' on that mismatch. Conversely, the single parents whose experiences allowed them to talk about homeless-ness and poor housing with some authority, felt that the programme was 'impartial', 'just stating an opinion'.

30.   SINGLE PARENTS
      (*KR*: It's a question of how the programme comes across in some ways. Is the programme on their side, or is it saying 'oh here's these poor victims . . . ?')
      I think it was impartial, wasn't it?
      It was just stating the facts really.
      It was just stating the facts, it wasn't giving an opinion.

But it does not follow from this that viewers whose discursive framework is in sympathy with that of the programme are necessarily blind to its mediated character. On the 'liberal' side of the argument, what it takes to trigger deconstructive readings is a degree of politicization with regard to the issues that the programme is dealing with, and also a familiarity with media practices which comes from being involved at the production level, rather than merely as consumers:

31.   CITIZENS ADVICE BUREAU
The media understand only too well as far as I'm concerned about Society's perception of the deserving and undeserving poor, because I know when they get in touch with us every winter, only in the winter, to borrow an old age pensioner to illustrate fuel poverty. And it's always a pensioner. And they always want the human interest element.

Later it is the same speaker who comments on the use of the disabled man (in an extract from programme 1 of *Breadline Britain* that I also screened for all the groups by way of introduction):

32.   CITIZENS ADVICE BUREAU
I don't remember seeing anything, any interviewer asking any of those people a question. And that made the programme better for me, because I'd rather see it from their point of view, and not the way . . .
(*KR*: Though there may have been questions)
Oh certainly yes I'm sure there was. 'Now you explain this', 'now you do this'. But it was more believable because they weren't asked questions. I thought the putting the shoes on bit was a bit over the top. And I thought, OK, the guy's been told to show the struggle coming down the stairs and all the rest of it, but it was still more believable. The stair scene was good but putting the shoes on was a bit over the top, even though we know he'd have to do that.

It is in the same group that a different speaker asks me whether the subjects were actors or real people; it is the same group that concur in suggesting that the programme would have been better if it had gone into the political background more, for example on housing policy; it is the same group that want more background information on the case histories because of their anxieties about other people's misperceptions about the poor. These viewers, more than any other group, stood at the interface between 'us' and 'them', and interpreted the programme accordingly.

Notes

1.   This differentiation between 'interpretation' and 'response' is a crucial one, though the importance of the distinction has only

recently begun to emerge in audience research. Briefly, the point is to distinguish the *primary* signification, the viewers' sense of what the programme is saying (and implying), from secondary matters such as their agreement/disagreement with that primary signification – indeed, in some cases, their critiques of how primary significance has been constructed.

2. There were actually two separate Townswomen's groups. The first group I interviewed were sisters and sisters-in-law, and I wanted to compare them with a less closely related group. But both groups reacted in very similar ways.

3. This formulation is too strong for plausibility if it is taken to imply a multiplicity of *discrete* meaning systems. This is most unlikely to be the case – the social domains which produce distinctive meanings are not hermetically sealed from one another. Then there are broad frameworks of understanding, like the liberal and conservative discourses on poverty, which can accommodate differentiated possibilities that nevertheless remain intelligible to one another because of what they have in common.

References

Corner, J. (1991) *Meaning, Genre and Context: The Problematics of a 'Public Knowledge' in the New Audience Studies.* London: Edward Arnold.

Corner, J., Richardson, K. and Fenton, N. (1990) *Nuclear Reactions: Form and Response in Public Issue Television.* London: John Libbey.

Dahlgren, P. (1988) What's the meaning of this? viewers' plural sense-making of TV news, *Media, Culture and Society*, 10 (3): 285–301.

Hoijer, Birgitta (1990) Studying viewers' reception of television programmes: theoretical and methodological considerations, *European Journal of Communication*, 5 (1): 29–56.

Jensen, K. (1986) *Making Sense of the News.* Aarhus: The University Press.

Lewis, J. (1992) *The Ideological Octopus: An Exploration of Television and its Audience.* London: Routledge.

Richardson, K. and Corner, J. (1986) 'Reading reception: mediation and transparency in viewers' accounts of a TV programme', *Media, Culture and Society*, 8 (4): 485–508.

Seiter, Ellen, Hans Borchers, Gabriele Kreutzner and Eve-Maria Warth (eds) (1989) *Remote Control: Television, Audiences and Cultural Power.* London: Routledge.

5 The beggar's blanket: public scepticism and the representation of poverty

Roger Hewitt

The parable of the beggar and the passenger

As I was going down into Euston underground station in central London I saw a disabled beggar who had propped himself against a wall with his 'homeless and hungry' notice. As I watched, another man – a passenger who must have passed by a little earlier – came along carrying a brown paper package which he thrust at the beggar hurriedly, and with some awkwardness, saying, 'Here you are. It's all fresh today', and quickly disappeared into the crowd. The beggar didn't speak but his face seemed to express amazement and anger simultaneously. The way in which the passenger uttered his words was with the forthright confidence of one who has emboldened himself to say something, did not want to be challenged and did not wish to engage in further dialogue to any degree. He had emerged suddenly from the crowd, spoken his words, then gone. For whose benefit was the gift?

At face value the passenger had decided not to give money but to give food – food chosen, perhaps, for its nutritional value. He seemed to have chosen to believe the notice that said the beggar was hungry. He seemed to have been so moved by the beggar's plight that he had actually gone to a shop, bought food and returned with it. He was a kind man. Most people pass beggars by. This man had taken some trouble. However, there was clearly more going on.

Even at the time, I heard the passenger's utterance as somewhat challenging, with the illocutionary force of: 'If you *are* hungry then you'll welcome this. If you don't welcome this then you're lying', and my evaluation chimed to some extent with the beggar's expression. The calculated absence of dialogue also seemed a prominent feature of this event. 'Speakers' rights' had been denied the beggar beyond that 'first utterance' of his self-presentation: disabled legs outstretched, body propped against the wall, 'h and h' notice, open cardboard box for collecting money. If this iconographic utterance was a 'first pair part' (request) the passenger's 'second pair part' (response) conclusively closed down the exchange. I'm not even sure if the passenger looked the beggar in the face. I don't know if he glimpsed the beggar's anger. So why was the beggar angry?

It seemed to me the beggar was angry because he rapidly read in the manner of the man's giving: 'If you mean what you say then take this.' The gift expressed both accusation and altruism tangled together. It had the aspect of a blow to the body: 'take this . . . and this . . .' Public scepticism had taken on dramaturgical form. It enacted two of the responses that potentially lurked in the minds of those who simply passed by. Furthermore, the beggar's impersonal request had evoked an equally impersonal – though totally non-usual – response, but it was as though this unusualness also needed no explanation or elucidation.

Not only was the beggar denied further 'speakers' rights', he was also denied the right to choose his own food. His preferences were deemed irrelevant in this act. 'Hungry' means you are supposed to need food. Your 'need' is potentially a matter of life and death – at least somewhere among its range of meanings. 'Preferences' and 'eaters' rights' do not enter into it. The beggar in this theatre existed only as empty mouth and stomach, was not individuated, was only his own icon. But he had asked for money to *buy* food. He had not asked for food. It seems to me that the passenger had stumbled into performing a foolish and fundamentally vicious action. He had also stumbled out of some mute dialogue with poverty.

In fact there is something profoundly dialogic about poverty in any social context. Its existence implies a response in a truly Bakhtinian sense – almost irrespective of its particular forms of representation. This is surely what Judas was onto when attempting to ensnare Jesus of Nazareth with his insistence that the woman who wished to bathe his feet with oil should rather give the money to the poor. Indeed Judas relied on the certainty that the constant and narrow 'answer' to the 'request' of poverty was to give and always only to give. His confidence betrays the basic social and human lineaments of poverty's representation that seem to have stretched throughout history and across cultures. It is not surprising to see the dialogue with this bedrock evident in Kay Richardson's viewers' groups – Townswomen's Guild, single parents, and so on – all part of a long historical conversation.

Jesus' answer has been a delight to the mean ever since: 'the poor are always with us', but that was not all he said. He also pointed his audience towards some warmer dimensions of the human predicament: to the truth of a generosity of symbols. It is the difference between funerals that have flowers and those where mourners are directed not to give flowers but instead to give money to a charity. Flowers are beautiful and do not last forever. That is the source of their symbolism at funerals. So the choice posed by a funeral is between the symbolic celebration of 'life in the face of the knowledge of death' (flowers) and the practical reasoning that says that such a use of flowers is 'wasteful'. The latter is a reasoning which does not recognize that it is its very 'wastefulness' that makes it able to be symbolic. And this was Jesus' point about the oil. He indicated another order beyond the bare threads of poverty, a denser cultural order of 'inner' truths, their signs and symbolisms. This, too, he implied, is a definitional human imperative.

There seems to be a trans-historical opposition of the basic, almost animal demand which poverty's existence is able to make, and Jesus' symbolical alternative. This opposition – the fundamental 'nature' in which the issue of poverty is embedded (the elementary social logic of survival) and the 'culture' of symbolic orders and their profligacy of signs – is apparent in a number of the viewers' responses to the sight of 'the poor' in *Breadline Britain*. Pressed by the insistence of poverty, the knuckle logic of the moral street-fighter is apparent in the viewers' discussions in numerous ways but none more Levi-Straussian than in the requirement that the poor stand categorically in the 'nature' column (selling their adornments to feed their children, for example) and vacate the 'culture' column completely. Like the personalized luxury of *choosing* what to eat, the wearing of jewellery and the smoking of cigarettes are part of a verdant social apparatus. The jewellery should fall off to leave, like Poor Tom in *King Lear*, 'a bare, forked animal' alone with the elements. It is as though these viewers were saying (and some of them *clearly* are): 'If you're *really* poor you don't wear jewellery, you don't smoke, you don't choose anything you consume' (Townswomen's Guild, groups 1 and 2, Chapter 4).

It is probably partly in recognition of this parsimony of interpretation that the self-representation of street beggars is usually so unadorned: the corrugated cardboard signs, the dogs on pieces of string and, above all, the blanket. Grimey, threadbare – sometimes it is a sleeping bag – the street beggar's blanket pulled up to the neck even in the hottest weather and passed on from hand to hand as a meagre 'resource' of the begging fraternity, must retain its simplicity. The signs of destitution must remain, themselves, basic. No embroidered, ethnic blanket will do. And if the 'material base' of this representational process practically guarantees its stark consistency, the spoken word must match it: 'Can you spare some change please?' Bursts of irony such as 'Can you spare two hundred thousand pounds please?' (middle-aged beggar, Euston Station, summer 1992) and unhumble insults, of course must stay as therapeutic asides only. They cannot be part of this text for public consumption.

As a regular London traveller and interested observer of begging exchanges I have been struck by the apparent futility of any representational strategy by the begging poor themselves. London's Victoria Station in rush hour, with its flocks of commuters waiting to read the announcements on the electric board, provides a site of instructive mass observation. Typically some one to two hundred people stand, necks craned upwards, as a hopeless figure, slightly below their horizon of gaze, makes his or her way through the crowd with a spare message and a cupped, upturned hand. I have watched this on numerous occasions but, alas, have been down on my observational luck in seeing even a single instance of giving. Compared with these beggars the representational semiotics of Euston's Underground are positively florid.

Usually, these beggars are unmistakably weather-worn street people. Twice I have seen apparently foreign beggars – once a dark-eyed, middle-aged woman with a middle-European headscarf, and once a pair of smudge-faced children – holding a scrap of paper with a handwritten message claiming to be in the first case a Rumanian (following the fall of the Ceausescus) and, in the second, from Sarajevo during some of the worst fighting. The note explained in each case that its bearer did not speak English, was a refugee and was destitute. There was something also very similar in the way the woman and the children moved, though I have no reason to believe they were connected other than by circumstance. They moved with a kind of bobbing, mechanical, resigned stiffness – head and neck rigid in relation to shoulders and chest, legs moving behind long, tawdry coats and cheap boots as though with little to do with the upper parts of their bodies. They moved as if they were performing some tedious task that had to be done but which they knew could not be accomplished. I saw nobody give them anything on either occasion. Either, therefore, public scepticism was unimpressed by their self-preservation, or they were believed but people saw no reason on that basis to give, or these waiting British Rail travellers had some principle about giving to 'official' charities but not to individuals, or maybe only giving to x number of beggars a day. It is difficult to tell. Whatever the variety of reasoning it produced a convincing uniformity of behaviour.

So what do they imagine about these beggars? One of the things that is believed is that they are, first, not really poor at all. It is all a con, a cynical manipulation. Only the easily fooled and those so soft that it impairs their judgement will be taken in by these displays. This is why the stories of the elderly poor with thousands tucked away in mattresses, and newspaper accounts of street beggars making £120.00 a day have such appeal. Things are not what they seem and 'I wasn't born yesterday'.

Indeed, there is something almost sadly anxious in this concern about being caught out, conned, taken in. As though each encounter is a test of their gullibility, their intelligence. Those who *are* seen to give are not, therefore, providing an implicit criticism of those who do not, but generously providing examples of those 'suckers' who are taken in, who *are* foolish, who are too soft for their own good. Those who give merely confirm the integrity of those who do not.

There is also something else that is avoided here besides the giving of cash. It is also what was excluded by the passenger who gave food, mentioned at the outset: a moment of one-to-one human contact that is potentially generative of complex feelings, even just for a moment. There is, in other words, an *intimacy of the moment of giving*, and it is this which is also pushed away.

Beggar and begged-from in 'face-to-face interaction'

What can be said of this 'intimacy of the moment of giving' itself? In India when you give to a street beggar they do not attempt gratitude. They all always register disappointment at the size of the donation – however large. In England giving to a street beggar used to provoke a stream of 'God bless you's, but whatever the context it seems there is always something in the exchange, some embarrassment, or something to negotiate, to get over which might overwhelm the moment. My own 'worst moment' of this kind was in India, at Krishna's birth place some miles south of Delhi when on a windy day and on an open square full of people, animals and glistening chaos, a begging woman, crouched at my feet, stretched out a hand to me for money. All of her fingers had been severed at the knuckle long ago. I had rupee notes which sat for a very brief moment in her palm before the wind snatched them away and we were overcome by the moment, embarrassment, my stupidity, her predicament and the pointless awfulness of it all.

These moments of contact between beggar and begged-from have their own structure of intimacy. I must confess a certain comfortableness with a stream of easily conferred 'God bless you, sir's, than with what has now emerged as the modern democratized counterpart – the chummy, 'we're-all-in-the-same-boat' sincerity of the thumbs-up sign and 'cheers mate'. I'm too conscious of the fact that we're not both in the same boat. But that's probably my problem. The relationship of beggar and begged-from seems to me to be intrinsically impossible to handle within a stable emotional framework.

Something of the contradiction and delicacy of this emotional framework is also glimpsed in the famous account given to Studs Terkel by an American hooker in his *Working*. The hooker explains about being paid to perform homosexual acts:

> The ethic was: You don't participate in a sexual act with another woman if a trick is watching. You always fake it. You're putting

something over on him and he's paying for something he didn't really get. That's the only way you can keep your self-respect.

The call-girl ethic is very strong. You were the lowest of the low if you allowed yourself to feel anything with a trick. The bed puts you on their level. The way you maintain your integrity is by acting all the way through.

(Terkel 1977)

This quotation, giving as it does an insider's view of another occasion in which intimacy and distance, authenticity and illusion are intermingled, may provide some insight into certain begging exchanges. It would seem, for example, that some beggars may need to tell *themselves* 'it's all a con', all an act. They themselves may not wish to face head on the reality of their begging, and they may develop strategies for the maintenance of dignity and self-respect which involve convincing themselves that they are in control, that they have their own 'hustle'. In this regard their view of what they are doing may coincide exactly with that of the sceptical traveller who 'won't be taken for a fool'. Both may be seeing it as a con and both could still be wrong. While the traveller will have some idea of what 'real' poverty looks like against which he or she supposedly measures each roadside mendicant, so too may the beggar. This may be especially true if the begger exists on the borderline of actual need which he or she manages in a day-to-day way. They may, in this case, engage privately with an *image* of poverty, either as a stereotype or as represented always by someone else not themselves, and thus 'know' that their public representation of poverty is an illusion for the punters. Like the sceptical traveller, they too, may be trapped within a set of well-established representations against which they see and interpret their own plight. Perhaps all beggars of this persuasion and the begged-from of the complementary persuasion, are locked into these representational structures *equally*, differing merely in their positions within the drama of the moment of giving.

In contrast, the chummy, 'we're-all-in-the-same-boat' approach may not only escape this representational web, it may be a better, more balanced response to being given to than either 'God bless you' or 'there's one born every minute'. Certainly it could be seen as a healthy, even moral way of maintaining self-respect while not denigrating the giver at all (as in the hooker's strategy) but also not elevating the giver beyond reason, according him or her instead this democratic acknowledgement – 'cheers mate' – genuinely felt.

Poverty writ large – scepticism and the media

If we look at some of the things said by one of Richardson's *Breadline Britain* viewers – a recruit to the research who had in the very recent past certainly been a poor street person himself – we find a mixture of these attitudes coming across.

> *KR*: Do you think that the label 'poor' is a label that people would shy away from to an extent?
>
> *P*: Yes, it's obvious isn't it? I mean anybody, you turn around and say to someone 'Oh, you're poor', and they're going to say 'No. I'm not that poor. I'm managing.' Do you know what I mean? If someone said to me I'd (say?) 'I wasn't this morning.' It's just something you wouldn't like to stick on yourself.
>
> *KR*: Yes but [. . .] the people in the homeless episode, for example, would you think, 'yes, they're definitely poor' or not?
>
> Pause.
>
> *P*: They're not begging enough.
>
> *KR*: They're not poor?
>
> *P*: No. I mean they're poor in terms of losing their housing, in terms of poor, somewhere to get a decent kip, but I mean, depending on what you can afford, people say, I mean in terms of money, I know loads of people in London who beg, right. I know loads of them. They're all pulling eight-ninety quid a day. It's, I'm not joking. That's not poor. They can go and book in a hotel. But not everybody's like that. I mean the ones who sit there and beg, I don't understand why they should, because there's food, they want food. And I don't mind people begging for housing, if they're going to beg up their money for a flat, [it's a way of getting] a couple of hundred pound. So if you begged up your money for a flat, got your flat, made your claim and started from there. But for some reason they don't, they get lost.

This account is more coherent than it may look at first sight. First, he is questioning the definition of poverty present in these issues. He is arguing that the homeless street beggars are structurally poor 'in terms of losing their housing' and 'somewhere to get a decent kip' but he is adding that in terms of the presence or absence of cash in the hand – without property, housing and other forms of underlying security coming into it – they may not be 'poor'. This is a gloss on his assertion that he knows London beggars who are 'all pulling eighty-ninety quid a day'. He adds that 'not everybody's like that', and indeed it does seem that there is great variation in both the amount of appeal some beggars have over others, and the value of particular begging sites. Central London stations are better than inner-city Underground steps. Some beggars sit all day and half the evening with hardly anything to show for it. Others will collect quite a lot of cash in a fairly short time. But even those who may collect most do not thereby become economically the same as those they collect from. 'Pulling eighty-ninety quid a day', even, does not translate into getting two thousand pounds a month within a stable lifestyle. The 'con', if such it be, of those who beg large sums and 'can go and book in a hotel' is thoughtfully re-interpreted and re-contextualized in this viewer's comments.

This viewer also has quite a different moral agenda from all of the others Richardson recruited. He feels that it is legitimate and comprehensible to beg enough cash to then get a flat from which address a social security claim could be made – i.e. begging to transform one's basic structural position. What he disapproves of is endlessly begging and getting 'lost' in a certain begging culture. This is certainly a moral view unlikely to be shared by viewers on any other of Richardson's panels, with the possible exception of the single parents group. It is, however, perfectly consistent with all of his other remarks – that what he saw in the programme he did not find shocking because it was so familiar, 'just normal'; that the programme was 'patronizing' in 'pigeon-holing people', their differences as human beings each managing differently in a tough world being lost in their documentary personae as 'the poor'; that nobody would think of themselves as 'the poor'. He also believes that certain episodes in the programme rested too heavily on an ironic contrast of the beggar and the begged-from:

It gave you time to look but didn't give you any time to think, to form an opinion about it. Just about all your opinion had was one given by the camera, like that bird sitting there going 'Got any spare change, please?' And someone goes into that house behind her, into that flat. I'm sure they done that on purpose, because she was sitting on the doorstep and someone walks into that flat and she's sitting there, homeless, and they didn't even look at her, and she's like that, just totally ignored her, that's all, she's there every day and it's part of life, there's nothing she can do about it and she went home to sit and watch her on TV. That's the kind of thing.

This panel member is a kind of limiting case. He is not typical of either a 'general viewer' or any of the members of the other panels involved in the research. And because the content of the programme was already so familiar to him he was not a target audience but, more accurately, eaves-dropping on a programme made for others – for those for whom it was unfamiliar. His criticisms of the programme are, however, instructive, and form part of a commentary on the responses of the others. In seeing the programme as representing a world he knew intimately he was able to locate:

1. strategies which permitted the sceptic a basis for criticism;
2. failures to truly represent the extent of the problems of poverty and homelessness;
3. dramatic simplifications which departed from the real basis and human texture of the issues for reasons of proselytizing and for technical motives.

The panel drawn from the single parents group was interesting because, in a sense, they represented the reverse of scepticism – not gullibility, but a strong commitment to what they took the programme to be showing. They had all experienced hardships of various kinds, mainly involving them in the negotiation of various social services and coping with the difficulties of single parenthood on a low income. In conducting the discussion with them it seemed to me that Richardson had some difficulty in getting them to engage with the issues about how the programme constructed poverty and homelessness because they were so concerned with the reality they saw the programme indicating. Indeed the reality the programme 'referred to' dominated their exchanges and the programme itself, in this collective viewing context, primarily triggered memories of experiences rather than induced, say, critical reflection. The analytical and diagnostic dimensions of the programme were almost invisible. It also served as providing exemplars in what was clearly for them an on-going struggle with authorities of various kinds. We find them at different points in their discussion, for example, citing engagements with the following bodies: the electricity board, the gas board, the Government, local councils, water authorities, housing departments and the Department of Health and Social Security (DHSS). Their position was that of an 'us' struggling against a 'them' of officials, bureaucrats and 'the well-off'. And they were far more explicitly political than any of the other groups:

> I think the deterioration's come with the Conservative Government actually, the deterioration of the standard of living, of the poor, has gone worse and it's still gonna get worse if we don't get rid of them.

For them the programme was a prompt for a kind of talk about life conditions. This was the kind of object it was, and if programme-making was visible at all it was in not going far enough: 'Things are even worse than what's shown.' Furthermore, their experience had led them towards an almost conspiracy-theory account of the workings of bureaucracies and this, too, affected, perhaps, their notion of programme-making:

> M: They're trying to brainwash you into a certain way of thinking, aren't they really? To see the programme in a certain light.
>
> KR: Well all programmes have accounts that they want to put across.
>
> P: Yes ... They're not going to put on certain things, to make it more emotional because they might get a throw-back on it. They might get into trouble for it. It's a possibility. If you'd seen the whole show before it was cut ...
>
> D: I'd think it would be more dramatic.
>
> P: ... you might have seen a bit more. But naturally you won't.

– the force of this 'naturally' tying the talk back to that shared experience of reality. It is also 'their' story in sharing the same reality in which they do daily battle with officialdom and struggle to make ends meet. 'Naturally' that reality is always suppressed in its fullness.

However, they, too, were strongly aware of the potential scepticism and resistance of others:

PS: All our sympathy doesn't count for anything because we relate to them. I'll give you an example. I was in the pub on Monday night, taxi driver pub, and they were talking about that programme on ITV, *World In Action*, and the taxi driver sitting next to us, he said 'What do you think of all these people begging on the streets and all that?' And he said, 'they're scum.' 'Parasites', he said, 'I'd lock them all up.'

D: How can they be parasites when . . .

PS: He's a taxi driver, he's earning a good living.
? Mm.
? That's how they look at it.

PS: His mate next to him said, 'How can you say that?' He said 'They're scum.' Now we all sympathize with them but the people who, the people that matter, the people that have the money don't want to know.

D: Don't care.

KR: Don't you think that if a person like your taxi driver friend saw that, that . . .

M: He has seen it.

D: They don't believe it.

PS: They call them parasites because they're begging on the streets.

S: They think they're there because of they've made themselves that way.

M: And they're lazy.

D: 'It's your own fault. You shouldn't 've got pregnant.' 'You shouldn't have left the home you were in.'

PS: The people they look to for sympathy don't want to know, you see.

KR: So you think the fact that everyone here is sympathetic isn't anything to do with the programme.

D: Because most of us have been there.

M: Because we've been through it.

The viewers cited so far from Richardson's research brought certain kinds of 'insider knowledge' to their reading of the programme they saw. Scepticism, if it existed at all, resided either in their critique of the adequacy of the programme to match the extremes of the reality they had experienced, or in matters of detail about the (undisputed) reality. It was not a scepticism about poverty or the nature of its representation. When we come to the Townswomen's Guild groups, however, we encounter a more complex tangle of attitudes, ideologies and consciousness of programme-making than in any of the above.

Two different groups of women participated on different occasions. One of these groups – Group 2 – was very unified in its response. Its members contrasted the poverty portrayed in the programme with what they had witnessed in the 1930s. They also unambiguously saw most of the people in the programme as to blame for their own plight. These they also read as representatives of a modern tendency to expect state support and general sympathy while lacking personal 'pride' and fighting 'spirit'.

The following quotations are typical of their response:

> I think some of them bring it on themselves. They don't particularly want to work. And some of them that have money, they spend it on the wrong things. When they do get their allowances they don't always spend it economically really.

And:

> G: I'll tell you something now. The poverty today is not the poverty there was fifty years ago. They were in rags then, weren't they. (simultaneous voices)
>
> G: Yes, but they were all proud. They were very proud people.
>
> L: They wouldn't let next door know.
>
> M: Oh no.
>
> G: It was pride. You had pride in your family.
>
> L: But I remember the running barefeet. (simultaneous voices)
>
> M: And the seat of their trousers out.
>
> A: Yes, yes.

It was nothing to see children barefoot.

M: Oh no.

G: And they were all happy ...

This is, of course, a familiar discourse among this generation and, like a popular song, they all join in on the chorus. However, its over-familiarity can obscure its profounder roots, and if we look carefully at what they say certain coherent and distinct notions begin to emerge. They are, for example, conscious of the fact that some people today also have 'pride'. However, when applied to people in the past – the golden age of pride and poverty – this concept emerges with a distinct shape and provenance. Most important is the attribute of self-reliance it seems to imply:

> I mean years ago you couldn't have gone to places like that. There was no such thing as those [Social Security] places. If you were poor, you were poor you got on with it.

'Getting on with it' meant managing the little you had to best effect:

> Do you know, my mother and father, they only got ten shillings a week pension in those days. That's all they got. And a big rent and everything else to pay for in those days.

In this *personal* management of poverty an underlying human spirit was glimpsed:

> I know a boy, he was brilliant. His parents were terribly poor. And he used to stuff all papers in his shoes. And he passed right through, here, university, got a degree and got everything. And he did marvellous, absolutely brilliant. I take my hat off to that boy. He used to go and sit in the doctors, where you could study. Nowhere else for him to go.

A similar emphasis on the resourcefulness of poor people in the past was also evident in the other Townswomen's Guild group (Group 1), with some interesting additions:

Well I was widowed at forty-two. And I had two children. And that was forty-nine. And I had to get a part-time job. I got no help from the state.

That's how I was.

Well my mother was widowed in the 1930s with three children and she was given ten shillings a week to live on.

That's right.

So that to me was poverty, she literally had to go out, well, she took in washing. And she had to hang it in somebody else's back yard in case the parish came and saw it in her back yard, they would think she was getting money or doing that and would take the ten shillings off her. Probably that's why I haven't got any pity when they put these things on. I watch them because I'm very interested in the reactions of people, and I think a lot of people, they've poverty of spirit, they've no spirit.

It is. It is.

And television always seems to pick on people like that who've got no go in them. Some people have, but they always seem to choose . . . As my grandmother used to say, they've got a face for getting the parish. I don't know whether you've heard of the parish or not, (simultaneous voices)
they seem to choose people like that. Or they choose people who are very aggressive, 'the world owes me a living'.

The concept of the poor person who has pride, is resourceful, manages in an improvisatory way with little to draw from, merges with the individualistic notion of 'spirit'. It is having 'go' and a plenitude of spirit that is the underlying moral quality accompanying pride. That people individually picked their way, daily, through the mass poverty and each made their own patch of survival, is what is being attested to here.

These kinds of views do, of course, constitute part of a certain kind of discourse about the past – one that cleans it up so that everyone survived, helped each other, smiled though their shoes were out, and so on, but its emphasis on the personal management of poverty in contrast to what these viewers regard as the television programme-makers' presentation of exemplars of need, distinguishes it as more than just an old song. Indeed, it chimes, to some extent, with some of the things said by the ex-street person quoted initially. He too, it will be remembered, saw the programme as dealing too much in *examples* of poverty and missing the fine grain and detail of the daily management:

> They're going to say, 'No. I'm not that poor. I'm managing.'

His view of poverty and the morality of survival is far indeed from those of the Townswomen's Guild, yet his intimate observations of daily life and the galaxy of characters he has known as they 'get by' at the bleak end of things, seems to occupy the same ground as their tales of simple economic heroism in the 1930s. His complaint of the programme 'pigeon-holing' people may be not that far removed from what the Townswomen mean when they complain that 'television seems to pick those people' who 'give the impression: I'm here. Feed me' – not in what it says about people but in what it says about the bowdlerization of individual lives in this chosen 'text' of the programme-makers.

Of course, these viewers are 'missing the point' of the programme, or rather, they are making it clear that they are not an appropriate audience for this text. In their own words, 'Maybe we're the wrong people to do this sort of thing because of how we grew up.' However, it is not their lack of sympathy for the modern poor as represented in this programme that disqualifies them, nor the singularity of their historical experience. It is the mismatch between their social and conceptual frame, and the academic, 'social-planning' approach organizing and generating the television text with its 'case study' – as opposed to 'life study' – material surface ordering and constructing the representation. It is a text generated from the 'wrong grammar' as far as they are concerned. They are concerned with the grain of individuated life. The 'social planning' discourse orders this material on quite a different axis so that while it appears to be 'readable' as 'just how things are', and therefore draws in a range of viewers – 'the film's there for everybody, aren't they, they're geared towards it' – there is, in fact, a tremendous cultural gap between text and audience in this case. It can be put simply as a mismatch of two discourses: a 'personal management of poverty' discourse and a 'bureaucratic management of poverty' discourse, but there are also issues of class location which affect *access* to these different discourses.

The ability to read the programme *was* evident to some extent in the Townswomen's Guild Group 1. In their talk, the 'personal management of poverty' discourse jostled with the 'bureaucratic management of poverty' discourse and they seemed, at times, to be engaging with the programme in a way that was at least related to that of the Citizens Advice Bureau panel. This latter group were, of course, not only very familiar with the issues dealt with by the programme, its members also had their own vocabulary for discussing it. They were professionals and the bureaucratic management of poverty was one of the areas in which they had specialized knowledge.

Their language was starkly different from that of the other panels. They spoke of 'policies', 'housing authorities', 'social conditions' and 'the 1986 Social Security Act'. They could provide a critique of bureaucratic details mentioned in the programme and they could say things like: '[The programme] didn't verbalize the link between health, housing, and income, and the fact that they're all separate departments. And I think that it's important that that is actually expressly said.' While some of the matters they mentioned were the same as those mentioned by other panels, they were distinguished by how they put it together, and the way they understood both how the system worked and how to act upon it and provide a critique with the judgemental confidence of someone equal, not deferential, to the system-builders.

Operating at the 'social policy' level is something outside the occupational and educational experience of the Townswomen's Guild panellists, but some of them in the first of the two groups did display something of an institutionally aware perspective. They produced sentences like: 'How do some people escape this net, this social security net?' or

> So with the situation we're faced with in, we need more hostels, don't they, more nursery places, and some provision for these people who are homeless. If they're in a hostel they've got an address and then they can get Social Security.

Their difference with the Citizens Advice Bureau was that they spoke as non-players in the game of influencing the workings of the system, and their utterances of this kind were found side-by-side with 'personal management' material:

The girl in the bed sit, she got two lots of ear-rings. I think, and quite a number of chains. If I was desperate for money, if I was in that position, I'd sell them, if they were worth anything, which I think today a lot of them are.

The bureaucratic discourse was emergent and its perspective fragmentarily present.

Access to this discourse and, more importantly, the cultural ground rules for its manipulation, seem to be shared by the Citizens Advice Bureau panel and the programme-makers almost alone. It is not surprising that Richardson found in the Citizens Advice Bureau panel's discussion a closer engagement with the aims and methods of the programme. There is often a class basis to the selection and readability of media texts and this programme, while seeming to invite all-comers, actually encoded a class culture in its organizational and conceptual grammar, and, in a sense, selected its 'real' audience through this underlying order.

Some of the Townswomen's Guild members clearly recognized the differences between their experientially textured sense of poverty and the theoretically foregrounded projection of the programme-makers. Curiously they even put this discrepancy in class terms, although they narrativized it in terms of sentiment:

I always think a lot of these programmes are made by, probably, middle-class, who've never known that sort of situation. And they feel more sorry because they're never known it. I don't know whether I'm right or not. There are working-class youngsters who go into the media now. But I always feel that it comes across, that it's put on the media by people who've never known it. And they probably feel more sorry than otherwise.

This panellist may or may not be right in the substance of what she says but she certainly seems to have intuited something going on behind the presented text, filtering it in ways that make class relevant.

Interestingly, for all of their affinities with the programme makers, some of the Citizens Advice Bureau criticisms of the programme were not unlike those of some of the other panels. All groups – except the Townswomen's Guild – were concerned with the gaps in the presentation of poverty that might allow the sceptical to find fault. (The Townswomen's Guild, as it were, proved their point.) For none of the groups was the programme regarded as distorting reality, although none credited it with any great polemical or representational success. Indeed, its earnestness seemed to have placed it beyond any extreme reaction from any of the panellists. For the non-believers of the Townswomen's Guild its makers were regarded much like the 'gullible softies' who give to beggars, as inexperienced about 'real life' and the no-nonsense pragmatism of the worldly.

This account of the programme's *innocence* in relation to its public is interesting. It was not seen as politically motivated – indeed some panel members complained of its lack of politics – and it was broadly regarded as simply descriptive. This contrasted sharply with its reception by sections of the press, as Ulrike Meinhof describes in Chapter 3. It would seem that once media presentations become the object of media attention, and the political stakes become raised, we encounter, in the case of poverty, something approaching a state of macro-scepticism.

This was illustrated even more clearly in the case of the NALGO advertisements, discussed by Brian Street in Chapter 2, which appeared during our sample week. During the very long 'run up' to the general election the NALGO union ran a series of full-page advertisements in the press, and a poster campaign designed to attack the Government's record of support for public services. The Tory popular press and the Conservative Central Office through it, denounced the advertisements in a series of newspaper articles.

As Street points out, one of the techniques used in this attack was that of unveiling the 'real truth' behind the images of need presented in the advertisements. The constant claim by the press to be directly reflecting reality, while clearly generating narrative, sets up a zone of paradox in which representational battles are played out. On the one hand their strategy of 'exposure' elevates the importance of 'reality', 'the world', 'the true' above the abstract, the general, the signifier, the 'politically motivated'. At the same time, readers are not led 'barefoot into reality' but, of course, merely shod in a different set of narratives. The press do not comprise, as it were, a clutch of jobbing nominalist philosophers rooting out and deconstructing 'universals' wherever they be found.

In part the battle over the NALGO posters was between the

photographic image and the printed word. The press' 'deconstruction' resided in taking NALGO's visual signifiers, giving them time off from semiosis, and getting them to speak directly to the public 'round the edge of the construction'. While the NALGO posters do not assume that people will treat the photographs as documentary evidence but as signifiers of a truth outside themselves, their political opponents treated them as deliberate illusions.

Journalists know, as do most media-literate people, that posters such as those used by NALGO, are produced by advertising companies using their normal professional means. The *Evening Standard* even included some allusions to this fact in their article. They reported:

> NALGO spokeswoman Mary McGuire denied the campaign was a complete sham but freely admitted that the four people used in the national newspaper series were models. 'Of course they are models' she said. 'That is what advertisers do. We could hardly have used real people suffering. That would be even more invidious.'

This explanation, embedded within a thicket of accusation, was followed by a paragraph reporting a foundational claim strategically not unlike that of *Breadline Britain*'s definition of poverty. Mary McGuire said:

> All our information is based on reliable sources such as government publications, the National Audit Office, independent experts and Hansard.

However, directly following this 'dull' appeal to academic truth, the *Evening Standard* continued by pulling 'reality' on stage from the wings in the form of Louise Vickery, the model in the education poster:

> The model in the school poster is Louise Vickery, a third year pupil at Clitter House junior school in Cricklewood, where headmistress Mrs Ann Edwards was furious today about the claims of a 'freezing and crumbling' school. She says her school is well-heated, in good condition and has plenty of teachers for the 150 pupils. (*Evening Standard*, 2.5.91)

By the time the drama of the article has slowed down the piece is allowed to close with:

Mr Mark Ratley, accounts director for Boase Massimi Pollitt, admitted they had used models to illustrate a general picture and not a specific case.

But he said this was exactly the same approach as used in the recent Government Aids adverts and the Department of Transport drink drive campaign.

Of course one does not need to be a semiotician to see the force of 'admitted' in the above quotation, as against other possible alternatives such as 'pointed out'.

It's not so much the dishonesty of the press that is of interest here – at least not in its moral dimension. It is the strange significatory field that it sets up. It is worth being clear about this: the writers of this article know that what they are doing in creating this narrative is building on a misconception – that the advertising company campaign 'implicitly' claimed to use documentary evidence, not models. They know that this is untrue, yet: (a) it makes 'good copy', and (b) it attacks the Government's opponents – and the paper supports the Government.

Truth is a common casualty in journalism but here, as with most of the stories in the other newspapers on this issue, we are somehow launched into a world of pure signification, that is not only 'truth' but 'meaning' also disappears – at least as 'reference' – and we have instead a kind of ideological froth in which empty signifiers crash against each other: a battle between unhinged elements. If ever there was a discourse loosed from all moorings this is it. Yet clearly it does a certain kind of work. It is a move in a very large ideological game with consequences on polling days, consequences for constituencies of interest, consequences for power. In Gunter Kress' terms, these are indeed 'motivated signs'.

What gives the journalists the hope that their fairly transparent mischief making will be read in the spirit it was intended is their reliance, not on public scepticism exactly but on the common tendency to look for the loophole in any communication concerning poverty or need. The justification for employing this fundamentalist psychology would, in this case, probably have to be provided at the broad political level. It would be justified in terms of party political battles for public opinion – 'a small lie for the sake of a big truth', or some such. But it also seems to take on a special kind of ferocity when the issue of poverty is involved. It is as though the unrefusability of poverty's demand is deemed to be so decisive that it is denied with special urgency.

I have dwelt on both Richardson's material and the row over the NALGO advertisements in an attempt to approach some of the conceptual and emotional tangles that poverty seems to generate once it is taken up into the public domain of media presentations. In fact it seems that the nature of scepticism changes very little at this level. What changes most of all is that it becomes manipulable for ulterior purposes other than those of personal self-defence. In the cases we have looked at, furthermore, the 'search-for-the-loophole' anticipatory nature of the 'poverty dialogue' was not written into these particular media texts – certainly in the case of *Breadline Britain* – with anything like a sufficiently low cunning to match the tabloid's grasp of the genre. Why was it, as Richardson points out in Chapter 4, that so many of her viewers' panels 'ventriloquized' the imagined sceptical others who might see the programme? Approaches about poverty to wide audiences need to start, as it were, in the thick of dialogue. Like the beggar who approached me recently with 'Can you spare some change? . . . I know I'm smoking . . . a roll up, but . . .' His smouldering cigarette and his request were already structured in a discourse of which he was acutely conscious. *Breadline Britain* could have done with more of this kind of 'street wisdom'.

Street Corner Society

I would like to conclude, where I began, with the street people. They are not, of course, all of the poor, but as one writer commented in 1853: 'The rich lose sight of the poor, or only recognise their existence by their appearance as vagrants, mendicants or delinquents' (Holland 1853) and their self-representations on this front-line are of special interest in contrast to media representations.

It seems to me that even in the abstract, politicized atmosphere of the media constructions, the recalcitrant irreducibility of poverty is always present beneath the fireworks, and we are constantly returned to that 'social contract' dimension, or rather to some Durkheimian pre-contractual state – the elementary stuff of poverty's pan-human challenge. Yet we are also somehow a long way from Wordsworth's notion of the important humanizing job done by the beggar who 'keeps alive the kindly mood in hearts' by giving others the opportunity to know that they have been:

> the dealers out
> Of some small blessing; have been kind to such
> As needed kindness for the single cause
> That we have all of us one human heart

(Wordsworth 1969)

For that there is no substitute for the real thing and 'the intimacy of the moment of giving' itself.

Here, the question of representation and the status and establishment of signs in this domain is clearly shot through with interactive considerations. In his *Behaviour in Public Places*, Goffman draws the distinction between signs 'given' by people in co-presence, and signs 'given off'. In other words representations intended and those that are uncontrolled. In begging exchanges, for example, the beggar's collecting utensil might be chosen for its pathos, while the beggar's pallor, due to un-nutritious diet, sleeping rough and poor general health, remains the unmanipulated base – the 'given off'.

Beyond this primary distinction, there is the exploitation of the 'given off' within some wider representational strategy. The 'conscious use of the genuine' is related to beggars' own 'con stories' and the web of representation both beggar and begged-from are entrapped by. This strategy – perhaps the most self-conscious example being the practice of certain Irish tinkers of taking their undoubtedly ill-looking children with them begging – is, of course, designed to do what all begging representations attempt to some degree: to get behind the scepticism they know their presence provokes. It is an attempt at an ultimate form of undeniable communication: 'Yes, this is a representation *and* it is documentary'; 'We are both "the real" and "the construction" '.

When even Poor Tom in rags on *King Lear*'s blasted heath is in
fact not just a 'bare, forked animal' but a disguised drop-out from
the aristocracy – Edgar, the Duke of Gloucester's son – it is not
surprising that the hard-working traveller needs to look twice at
the pasty-faced street beggars. However, the invaluable semiotic
resource of extreme pallor is likely to remain for the homeless for
some time. Illness and bad health due to poor diet and inadequate
shelter is greatly increasing among them, especially among the
young, and tuberculosis is common now again. While I was
buying a coffee at Victoria station a young woman of disturbing
complexion stood beside me and said simply: 'Buy me something
to eat.' 'Would you like one of these?' I said, pointing to a ham-
filled croissant. 'Anything', she said. 'Or these?' 'Anything.' The encounter was every poverty-sceptic's dream: a beggar begging not
for money but for food and not minding *what* food. Furthermore,
had I chosen to I could have probably actually observed her eating
it. It was the reverse of the encounter between the traveller and the
disabled beggar described at the beginning of this chapter. It was
almost, too, that Euclidean ideal: poverty without representation.

Finally, to move the discourse back from charity to flowers, one
aspect of poverty that has only briefly been touched on here is the
issue of verbal communication. It is no coincidence that the classic
studies of homelessness, the Chicago school ethnography, *The
Hobo*, by Nels Anderson (1924) and George Orwell's *Down and
Out in Paris and London* (1932) both have quite a lot to say
about talk and communication generally, and its importance to
street people. This is an issue which also arose in the interview
with Richardson's ex-street person. There he said:

> To me, poor's like being alone, with nothing, being on the road
> without . . . no-one to talk to you, you know, that's poor. But you're
> in a B and B and your family might be in the same area, at least
> you've got somewhere you can go and talk, and you're not so poor
> really. You can cope better with it then.

A friend who works with homeless and semi-homeless drug
addicts kindly interviewed several of her clients for me about
begging, which was one of the survival strategies often used by
them. Their observations have informed this chapter in a number
of places. One unanimous observation, however, was that they did

not mind people not giving but what they hated was people not speaking. Those who gave but who did not speak were, from their point of view, nearly as bad as those who neither spoke nor gave. Those who did not give but who spoke were much appreciated. This does not apply, of course, to abuse, of which they receive a great deal. The guillotine on discourse used by the food-giver in the account at the start of this chapter was exactly an affront in this sense. Perhaps for the city traveller this could point to the representation of a new kind of affluence – and to the possibility of talking your way to heaven.

References

Anderson, N. (1924) reprinted (1962) *The Hobo*. Chicago: Chicago University Press.

Holland, C. G. (1853) The vital statistics of Sheffield, p. 51; cited in Thompson, E. P. (1968) *The Making of the English Working Class*, Harmondsworth: Penguin, p. 356.

Orwell, G. (1932) *Down and Out in Paris and London*. London: Victor Gollancz.

Terkel, S. (1977) *Working*. London: Peregrene, p. 80.

Wordsworth, W. (1969) Wordsworth Poetical Works. Oxford: Oxford University Press, pp. 444–5.

Index